Women of the Red Year

Women of the Red Year
Two Personal Reminiscences by British
Women of the Indian Mutiny, 1857

Reminiscences of the Sepoy Rebellion of 1857
Miss Florence Wagentreiber

My Recollections of the Sepoy Revolt
Mrs. Muter

LEONAUR

Women of the Red Year
Two Personal Reminiscences by British Women of the Indian Mutiny, 1857
Reminiscences of the Sepoy Rebellion of 1857
by Miss Florence Wagentreiber
My Recollections of the Sepoy Revolt
by Mrs. Muter

FIRST EDITION

First published under the titles
Reminiscences of the Sepoy Rebellion of 1857
and
My Recollections of the Sepoy Revolt

Leonaur is an imprint of Oakpast Ltd
Copyright in this form © 2019 Oakpast Ltd

ISBN: 978-1-78282-836-5 (hardcover)
ISBN: 978-1-78282-837-2 (softcover)

http://www.leonaur.com

Contents

Reminiscences of the Sepoy Rebellion of 1857

Contents

Introduction from Memoirs of Colonel James Skinner, C.B.

The name of Colonel James Skinner or" Sikander" as the natives called him (the *sobriquet* being given him by the men of his own Regiment, who compared him to Alexander the Great) is universally known throughout India as one who took an active part in the most stirring events of our early struggles in the country, and fought his way through that disturbed period—a true "Soldier of fortune"—and won renown and the success he so richly deserved.

There were few whom duty or business led to Delhi or Hansi (the headquarters of his regiment) that did not in some manner experience his kindness and hospitality. His warm-hearted liberality and generosity seldom failed to gain him the love and friendship of those with whom he had any intercourse; while his enterprising gallantry and indefatigable zeal always secured the praise of his military superiors.

Thrown in early youth amongst scenes of high excitement, daring and adventure—of military pomp and eastern magnificence j at one time struggling with danger, privation, and fatigue— at others revelling in the short-lived profusion, and reckless enjoyment purchased by victory and success, he became the creature of the times and circumstances in which his precarious life was passed; and even when the changes in his eventful career brought him back into contact with his countrymen, there still hung around him an air of barbaric splendour acquired by his Asiatic habits which invested him with an interest that few failed to sympathise with as striking and attractive.

No one, indeed, especially those possessed of any military enthusiasm could look upon old "Sikander" at the head of his fine corps of horsemen, his "yellow boys," as they were named from their yellow uniforms—and witness their martial air as they careered about in their wild and rapid manoeuvres, without admitting that they were a gallant band—that as irregulars they were unequalled in India, and that the leader and men were worthy of each other.

Few were more deeply imbued with real Christian feeling and charity; but thrown as he was at a very early age into a career of incessant activity, and chiefly amongst people of other creeds, it can scarcely be imagined that his notions of religion were as strictly orthodox and well understood as if he had remained entirely in Christian society until a more mature age. But the good soil was there, nor was the good seed wanting. He had his Bible, and he read it in the meek and earnest simplicity which was so much his characteristic. Even the society of the more respectable natives around him served to nourish his innate piety. For seeing them zealous in their own religion, mistaken as it was, he felt that he should not be the less so in the superior faith in which he had been born and bred.

As years rolled on, and his intercourse with European society increased, and quieter times gave more leisure for thought and reflection, the religious bent of his mind had more play to operate freely. He read and conversed more with those qualified to instruct him; and that he had done so with effect, and made progress in the doctrines of the British Church is certain, since he was confirmed by the bishop in 1836, at which time also his church was consecrated.

Amongst the chief objects which he desired to accomplish and which he at length attained was the erection of this Episcopal Church (St, James') built in token of a votive promise made when lying wounded on the field of battle near Oonearah.

It has been said that Colonel Skinner, when he purchased his house at Delhi, found in the compound or enclosure, a mosque in ruins, which he repaired, and this having given rise to some remark, he declared that though he respected Mohomedans, and would be the last to destroy, or desecrate their places of worship, he reverenced his own religion far more, and would prove it if God preserved his life, and he became rich enough to build a Christian Church. He did live, for when relieved by the Chamar woman who gave him bread and water, in the feeling of gratitude to providence for this unexpected succour at Oonearah the vow to build the Church was made and duly fulfilled.

He died at Hansi in 1841 and was buried with military honours at that place, but as, during his illness prior to his death, he had expressed a desire to be buried *under* the principal entrance to the Church "So that all persons entering might tread on the dust of the chief of sinners" the remains were disinterred on the 17th January of the same year and escorted by the whole of the corps and a great concourse of people to a place four miles from Delhi called Seeta-ram-ka-Serai where the cortege was met by all the Civil and Military Officers of the station, with a great multitude from the city—"None of the Emperors," said the natives, "were ever brought into Delhi in such state as Sikander Sahib," and an eye witness declared that he never on any occasion saw such a crowd.

A funeral sermon was preached over the body, at which all the Europeans at Delhi attended, and sixty-three minute guns, denoting the age of the deceased, were fired, and on the 19th of January the veteran soldier was committed to his final resting place. Those who stood by his grave could not help thinking of the conversations they frequently had about death, and the striking opinions he always expressed and maintained on that subject:

> We are just like seed which vegetates when cast into the earth; and we return from whence we came.

My mother was the youngest daughter of Colonel James Skinner. (*The Recollections of Skinner of Skinner's Horse* by James Skinner is also published by Leonaur).

Colonel Skinner had five sons and two daughters—of his sons the eldest (James) entered the army at an early age and served under his father in "Skinner's Horse."

The second (Hercules) served under the Nizam of Hyderabad as Captain in one of his Regiments. The three others (Joseph, Thomas and Alexander) remained with their father helping him with his estates and *Zemindari* work which was extensive.

The two daughters married officers in the British Army—Louisa, the eldest, married Captain James Turner, Royal Artillery, and the youngest of all the children Elizabeth (my mother) Captain Radclyffe Haldane, who was at the time in "Skinner's Horse," and who was killed some years after the marriage at the Battle of Chillianwalla (Sikh Wars).

My mother's early life was spent at Hansi amid strange surroundings. Her mother was a native of India and confined to the *purda* (as is the eastern with natives of rank and caste). The daughters were allowed to do as they pleased. To run wild with no one to check or interfere with them in any way—Elizabeth (Bessie) who had very little in common, or sympathy with her mother, and disapproved of the

13

restraint put upon her when in her society—spent most of her time out of doors, indulging in the sports and pastimes of her brothers; riding the wild unbroken colts in the paddocks; going out on an elephant after big game with her brothers; learning from them to shoot, to use the spear, to hunt and to drive.

Thus, she inherited an independent and ungovernable spirit, combined with utter recklessness or dread of danger, and many were her exploits and escapades at an age when most girls are in the school room with their minds in book-lore. Her father spoilt her, and turned a deaf ear to all complaints brought to him of her misdoings and disregard of discipline. This fearlessness led her into many a scrape, and on several occasions nearly cost her her life, but her father, proud of her spirit, upheld rather than checked or subdued it.

One day the child was brought to him while she was holding a Darbar cut and bleeding from a bad fall she had received from a horse she had been forbidden to ride. Instead of the punishment she so richly deserved she was placed upon a table and told to stand upright for all to behold the "child who had the soul of a second Sikander!"

Thus encouraged, when she merited disgrace and displeasure, nothing daunted her, or was too risky for her to attempt. The only one of the household she had any awe of was her eldest brother James who often punished her for her misdoings, incurring their father's displeasure thereby.

She was small and slight for her age and looked four or five when she was really double the age. This gained for her, from the servants, the name of *Chouia* or mouse.

In the hot trying summer time, when doors are closed all day, and houses kept cool with "*tatties*," "*pankhas*" and thermantidotes, even then her spirits never wearied or flagged, her restless activity pervaded the house making the noonday *siesta* an impossibility to the others. Her brother, worried with constant complaints, at length thought of a plan that would keep her quiet for an hour or so during the excessive heat of the day. She was coaxed into his room and made to lie down on the bed, while his pet tiger mounted guard over her. Thus, she remained quiet for an hour, the great beast beside her, his paw across her body, not daring to move and pretending to sleep.

Familiarity breeds contempt is a very true saying and in time the fear of the animal diminished. So that one day she gave his tail a good tug. Enraged and insulted, the creature turned savagely upon her, with a roar that roused the house, and had it not been for the timely interference of her brother her career would have ended then and there. As it was poor Bahadur (the tiger, who had been reared as a tiny cub in the house, and was as gentle and domesticated as a tame cat) had to pay the penalty end forfeit his life, for he was now considered dangerous, and was poisoned.

At the age of twelve it was thought fit to send her to school. So the two girls were sent to a good boarding school in Calcutta (the journey from Hansi to Calcutta was a matter of months and not hours, for there were no railways in those days) and left there in charge of a good worthy English lady who soon tamed her ungovernable spirit, and when some years later the sisters returned to Hansi, good looking, gentle mannered and accomplished it was hard to realise that they were the two wild untutored, little things that had left them a few years back. As may be imagined they were not destined to remain long under their father's roof.

Colonel Skinner was now a wealthy landowner and had retired from the service. Most of his time was spent at Hansi, paying occasional visits to Delhi and Bilaspur (where his *jagir* villages lay). At these places he had splendid houses where he lived in pomp and magnificence, kept open house and entertained all the great people who visited India in those days.

★★★★★★

Some years after her first husband (Captain Haldane's) death my mother came to reside with her brother Joseph Skinner in Delhi in the fine old house opposite the church which belonged to the Skinners. She had six children by this marriage. The two eldest sons were sent to England to be educated; one died and the three daughters remained with her. It was in those days that she met my father, George Wagnetreiber, and married him and had three children by this marriage.

George the eldest died a year before the Mutiny (shortly after I was born) and my youngest brother Bertie was born some years after the Mutiny.

I was a little over a year old when the Mutiny broke out, and, of course, too young to have any recollection of the event and the terrible days that followed, but my parents often spoke of their desperate fight for life on the night of the 11th May 1857, and all that happened after we returned to Delhi, and I have tried to describe the facts as plainly as I can remember them.

Our Escape from Delhi

"Coming events cast their shadows" they say, and the mutiny was certainly not without its warnings to many, though few, if any, attached importance to these. Strange and mysterious signs passed unheeded which were precursors of the trouble that was pending.

There was evidently a feeling of discontent, disquietude, and unrest among the natives—an undercurrent at work, which boded no good to the British rule in India; none, however, but those who had any knowledge of the subtlety of the Indians, their prejudices, and superstitions, could see through them. Thus it came about that while my mother, who was gifted with an insight into their character, realized that there was something wrong—some premeditated evil at work, some plot ripening, could do little to persuade others to share her belief, though she did succeed in convincing her husband that things were not as they should be.

These convictions were strengthened and nurtured by some remarkable occurrences which were foretellers of the event, which happened, however, when it was too late to avert the evil which followed, demoralising us so thoroughly and costing us so many valuable lives.

The house we were living in stood in civil lines below the ridge. It had extensive grounds which were, at the time, being laid out into plots, where fruit and other trees were to be planted in due course. At the farther end of the compound, close to the boundary wall, where the ground was slightly elevated and there was a good *pucca* well, a site had been marked out for a small cottage which was to be built there. A number of workmen were busily engaged in clearing the spot, preparatory to laying the foundation for the cottage.

One morning there was a terrible uproar among the *coolies* and my father, thinking they were wrangling and quarrelling, instead of setting about their business, sent a *chaprassi* out to tell them to "stop the row, or he would bring his whip to bear upon them."

Instead of this having the desired effect, the noise continued; so, taking up a light cane he hurried out to see what it was all about. Directly they saw him, the head *mistree* rushed up to him and fell prone at his feet, entreating him to give up the idea of building on that spot for "no house there will ever have a tenant!" My father was new to the country, and did not understand the language, so he sent the *chaprassi* to fetch the *Mem Sahib* to explain to them that he wanted the little place finished soon, and they were to set to work at once (for he had gathered that there was some demur about it).

At the sight of the *Mem Sahib* the *coolies* cried out that they "would not go back to the accursed spot unless my parents accompanied them!" When they arrived on the scene, the rest of the men were sitting about looking rather scared. The *mistree* led my parents to a deep hole in the centre of the square, from which they had been digging up stones, and they were surprised to see a flat, smooth, granite slab some three feet long, and as wide, deep down in the hollow.

"Why don't you remove the stone and see what is under it?" my mother asked, but they hung back and begged her not to interfere with it but to choose some other more favourable spot.

As she was curious to see what was beneath, she ordered some of the workmen to lift it with their pickaxes. They came forward with much reluctance to do as they were told, and when the stone was raised, they saw to their horror an enormous serpent! With coil upon coil the reptile lay, petrified in its snug retreat. My father would have shot it, but the men entreated him to spare it and it would go away of itself. They asked for two *rupees* to do *pooja* over it, which was given them, for my parents were curious to see what effect the *pooja* would have on the loathsome creature.

One of the *coolies* ran off to the bazaar, returning in a little while with sundries he had purchased with the money—powders of various colours, sandal wood, and *ghee* (clarified butter); they then proceeded to light a fire near the hole, and mixing all the ingredients together they threw them into the fire. Instantly there was a huge blaze, while it lasted, and till it burned itself out they prostrated themselves before it, chanting rhymes and incantations to the serpent deity—while the reptile raised its head slowly and glided into the rocks and jungle beyond. Then they went back to their labour in a more contented frame of mind, but the *mistree* informed my mother that she had disturbed a *grave* and the spirit of the *peer* (saint) had taken the form of a snake to scare away those who were disturbing its rest!

The house was never finished, for very shortly after, the mutiny broke out and the workmen absconded. After this came a request from the king's palace to allow one of the young princes (Jiwan Bukt), the king's youngest and favourite son, to practise target shooting in our compound with the Enfield rifle which was a source of much disaffection amongst the troops at the time. This seemed a strange request, and my mother had her suspicions about it; so, the prince was politely made to understand that a private compound was not a suitable place for such dangerous sport, and he must seek some other ground for the purpose.

In spite of the rebuff, a day later, came a splendid present from the king. Laid out on a silver tray, covered with a gold embroidered cloth, was a beautiful *mahseer* (fish). We afterwards learnt that five gentlemen had received these favours, *viz.*, the Resident (Mr. Fraser), Revd. Jennings (Chaplain), Mr. Le Bas (Judge), Sir T. Metcalfe, and my father.

Never having received any previous attention from the palace, my mother declared that the fish was *poisoned* and had it thrown away.

Shortly after, another overture of friendship was made from the same quarter. This time Jiwan Bukt sought an interview with my father. He was to come *veiled*, and at night, and my father was earnestly requested to see him alone. Again, he was foiled, for, since my father could not talk the language, he needed an interpreter, and my mother who really wanted to be on the spot if anything occurred, remained in the room all the time. Nothing unusual occurred. The prince was most civil and courteous and made no allusion to the unsettled state of things, nor did he give his reasons for wishing to see my father alone, at night, and *incog.!*

My uncle, Captain Skinner, who was at Hyderabad, often wrote about the strange rumours current in Hyderabad at the time. His orderly told him if he valued his life to take leave and go to Europe till the *trouble* was past; upon his asking the nature of the trouble, the man replied "a massacre of the *Feringees*" (white folk). My uncle told him there were many other *Feringees* who would speedily avenge the deaths of their countrymen out here and sent him about his business!

On the night of the 10th May, an old *nawab* who occasionally visited my father, called, and during the course of conversation, warned him that the 3rd Light Cavalry intended mischief, some of them having been imprisoned for insubordination to their officers on parade. He said "such stringent measures were tyrannical and foolish at such a time, and the Government would rue their policy." My father told him that he thought the troopers deserved death, not imprisonment, for showing such a spirit, and the sentence in his opinion was far too slight and lenient for such an offence.

All that could be done was done to acquaint the authorities of the disturbed state of affairs. The night of the *nawab's* visit a letter was sent off to Sir T. Metcalfe, begging him not to make light of it for the warning was evidently not without some cause; but Sir T. Metcalfe paid no heed, and at daybreak the next morning the mutinous troopers were crossing the bridge-of-boats, and their first victim was an unfortunate overseer who had gone out to his work across the river and whom they at once cut down and then rode into the city. It was then too late. The storm had burst! We were driven from our homes, and many were cruelly put to death while attempting to escape.

Early on the morning of the 11th a report prevailed outside the city that some troopers of the 3rd Light Cavalry stationed at Meerut had entered through the Calcutta gate of the city and were murdering Christians on every side, and committing all sorts of excesses. The reports varied as to the number of the troopers—by some they were said to be 250 whilst others estimated them at 15. The *Delhi Gazette* Press, where my father's work lay, was near St. James' Church (inside the Cashmere gate) his office hours from 7 to 10 a.m., every alternate day, and after breakfast to 4 pm., on the other days. This was fortunately a late day—had it been otherwise, he would certainly have shared the fate of the other poor Europeans in the city. He had just driven off, when our servants came up in a body, and asked to be allowed to go to their homes, as there was an uproar in the city.

This was unusual, and my mother guessed what it meant. Their sudden desertion, and wish to absent themselves in a mass, alarmed and convinced her that some serious trouble had to be faced. She harangued them, and told them they were to remain at their posts till the *Sahib* returned. Some of the old ones consented to stay, and the bearer was despatched forthwith after the office *gharry* to bring him back at all costs. The message given was to say "The *Mem Sahib* was very ill, and desired his immediate return." The bearer caught the carriage up at the Cashmere gate, which was closed. My father had alighted from the *gharry* and was pacing in front of the gate in a towering passion, inquiring of the Residency *Sowars* on guard, by whose authority the gate was closed, and demanding them to open it without further delay.

The bearer delivered the message, urging his immediate return as

"The *Mem Sahib* was quite unconscious and very ill." This was the saving of his life, for once the gate had closed upon him, he would never have returned. At the house all was alarm and confusion. My mother had worked herself into a frenzy during his absence, having learnt much of the truth from the servants, and was greatly relieved to see him safe and sound. Even then it was hard to realise the extent of the danger, the seriousness of the outbreak, and all it meant to us.

My father sent a note across to a neighbour (Doctor Balfour) asking for some particulars of the disturbance and advising him to bring his family over to our house which, having a tiled roof, was less likely to prove combustible. Doctor Balfour replied that there was no cause for alarm and that it would be advisable not to show signs of anxiety. Meanwhile the servants were busy bringing news from the city. The troopers were said to be like fiends, shooting down Europeans without mercy, and not even sparing the women and children—the commissioner (Mr. Simon Fraser) being one of the victims.

My father got his firearms together, loaded them all, and removed them into a good-sized room, having determined to retreat to this, and resist any attempt that might be made on our property. Firing could now be heard in the city, and a lurid glare over the tree tops in the direction of Duryaganj corroborated the statement that the residences of Europeans were being plundered and burnt after the inmates had been ruthlessly put to death. It was now ascertained that the troopers from Meerut were the prime movers, and were calling on the city people to join them in their brutal work of destruction. With the knowledge that revenge was their principal object, and the certainty that they were acting more like demons than men, matters assumed a serious aspect and my parents agreed to seek safety in flight.

Meanwhile the deadly work was going on in the city. It was said that the 54th Native Infantry had proceeded from cantonments to the city to quell the disturbance accompanied by two guns from Captain De Tissier's Battery. These had marched through the Cashmere gate and main guard in order, but just opposite the church, the *sepoys* of the 54th rushed to one side suddenly leaving their officers in the middle of the road; at the same time a small party of the troopers galloped forward and pulled up short, fired at the ill-fated officers and shot them down. The only one who had firearms was Captain Ripley, and he managed to kill (or wound) two of his assailants before he himself fell mortally wounded. The remainder, Captains Smith and Burroughs and Lieutenant Edwards were then coolly pistoled, their men calmly looking on at the butchery, and when ordered to fire, making a display of doing so over the heads of the murderous troopers.

As soon as the troopers had shot down all the officers, they dismounted, and going up to the *sepoys* shook hands with them congratulating them on their forbearance. The other regiments in garrison were then sent down with two guns, but it became evident that their presence at the scene of action only increased the dangerous nature of the outbreak, as things were in a state of open mutiny.

The treasury and bank were attacked and plundered; the *dâk* bungalow, with several other houses near it, burnt down. Two travellers at the bungalow (names unknown), Doctor Dopping, 54th Native Infantry, Mr. Galloway (Assistant Magistrate), Chiman Lall (Christian convert), the Berresford family, Revd. Hubbard, Mr. Sandys (Missionary), the Collins and Staines' families, and several others were foully murdered. The city people vying with the *sepoys* in acts of cruelty and destruction, and in most cases being the principal perpetrators, while the low caste *Chamar* women living about the Cashmere gate busied themselves looking for concealed Christians, and robbing the houses from the wall shades to the floor cloths.

The *Delhi Gazette* Press, College and all public offices were set on fire or battered down; the troopers calling out that "they were not seeking *loot* but life," and where they were disappointed in their greed for blood they let in the city *badmashes* who in the space of an hour cleared out the best regulated houses. They then either set fire to them, or if they were not of an inflammable nature, pulled out the doors and windows, and in some cases the beams from the roofs. In the church the ruffians found ample employment. They tore the monumental slabs from the walls, stole the plate, and after tolling the bells in mockery for a time, they loosened them and let them fall into the church below. The city gates were closed and barricaded so that no one could escape from the city. The proclamation being *Mulluk Badsha, hukkum Sepai!* (The country is the king's by the will of the *sepoys*). Had it not been for several acts of kindness and mercy rendered by individuals (in one or two instances by *sepoys* themselves) not one Christian in the city would have lived to tell the tale.

Our position in our own house now was extremely hazardous, and as it was said that all the residents in civil lines had gone to the brigadier's house in cantonment. we followed their example, taking only a small supply of necessaries, and firearms, avoiding the main road as unsafe and driving over the ridge. On the way parties of *sepoys* mounted on gun carriages passed us. My father asked them "where the brigadier and officers were." They replied "Go, and find them," and went their way singing out taunts and jests, mocking and reviling us till we were out of earshot. The miserable beggar brats about, ran after the carriage pelting stones at us, and loudly calling on us to *salaam* to them.

On reaching the brigadier's house the servants informed us that the brigadier was not at home, and the other parties who had come there to seek refuge had all gone, whither they knew not (or did not choose to tell us), so we turned homewards in despair. At our gate we were accosted by a neighbour (Mr Murphy) who begged us to go over to his house which was a good sized *pacca* one, which we did very gladly. Here assembled were a party of eight or ten ladies and six gentlemen. The latter were well armed, so it was agreed that we should make a stand here as long as we were able to hold out.

It was now about 12 noon. At the house there was a guard of *sepoys*, but their sullen look betrayed the true state of their feelings towards us, and it was only too evident that these were only biding their time. The reports from the city were sad and discouraging, so much so that the gentlemen consulted together as to whether it would be wise to barricade the house and remain in it, or follow the rest of the fugitives to the Flag Staff Tower, on the ridge, whither they were supposed to have gone.

Doctor Balfour and another gentleman went to the top of the house to watch the city gates. One brave fellow made a start for Meerut on horseback, but it is doubtful if he ever reached the bridge across the river—he was never heard of again.

About 2 p.m. Doctor Balfour came down, in a great way, to say that the troopers were swarming out of the Mori gate, and making straight for civil lines, and there was necessity for immediate flight. So, it was arranged to make a move at once. The tower was about a mile from the house. The heat was almost unbearable in the rooms. Outside, in the blazing sun, with the wind blowing like a furnace blast, it would be a terrible drive, but there was no other alternative. Conveyances were called for; we were put into them and the whole party set off once more for the ridge. Mr. McWhirter (one of the gentlemen) who had been suffering from fever was so overcome that he never reached the tower.

Here we found a large gathering from civil lines and the houses nearby—mostly ladies and children and their attendants (*ayahs* and bearers, carrying infants), all huddled together in the interior of the tower (a space some eighteen feet in diameter). Many of the poor ladies were in a terrible plight owing to extreme terror and the excessive heat.

Some had little ones who were crying and clinging to them which they were vainly trying to soothe and comfort. All wore that expression so near akin to despair. Here were wives made widows in one short hour, sisters weeping at the report of a brother's death, and there were those whose husbands were still on duty, in the midst of peril, of whose fates they were as yet ignorant. It was a sight not to be forgotten. A "black-hole" in miniature; all but the last horrible features of that dreadful prison!

There was not a tree near the tower to shelter it from the blazing noonday sun, and the little air that came in through the narrow doorways was scorching hot, the walls and stone floor baking like an oven. Wet handkerchiefs were bound round aching heads, but in spite of the utter helplessness and misery that prevailed, the stronger willed were endeavouring to bear up bravely, to encourage and comfort those who knew the worst, and had nothing to hope for, for their loved ones were to return to them no more. Pointing down the slope at the tower, and facing the city, were two guns of the Light Field Battery, and to the right, a company of the 38th Light Infantry with piled arms, and glittering bayonets. These only increased the terror of the poor women on that awful day, for they knew not at what moment those cruel weapons might be turned upon them and their helpless babes. The gentlemen of the party stood about the doorways (to give room inside) in groups There with loaded guns, seeking the little shade the Tower afforded, they watched and waited.

A little before 3 p.m. our bearer came up to ask my mother if she wanted a carriage sent up (ours had been sent back from Mr. Murphy's house); he was told to send the phaeton, and pair of young thoroughbred mares at once and also some food. Fortunately, the carriage had arrived when the need came upon us, or I do not know what would have become of us! Meanwhile the brigadier and my father went up to the guard. The former addressed them, while my father stood close by, gun in hand, facing the city.

The brigadier tried to reason with the men; he reminded them of their good services in the years that were past, and told them it would be well to their interest to remain staunch and loyal to their oath and the salt they had eaten for so many years. They immediately showed their distaste for the "salt" by expectorating about in a disgusting and disrespectful manner; one who seemed to have influence called out "Don't listen to the *Boorao!*" (old imbecile) and were altogether so insolent and offensive in their replies that it was evident nothing was to be gained by reason and argument.

While this was going on my father observed a cloud of dust on the road leading from the city, which turned out to be a crowd approaching rapidly, shouting, and making a great noise as they neared the tower. At the foot of the slope they paused, (and my father feeling sure that the row they made would create a panic in the tower), made a movement towards the cannon. The rabble, thinking they were going to be fired upon turned and fled helter-skelter, tumbling over each other in their anxiety to get away; but their cries of *Már Feringee!* had so unsettled and disorganised the *sepoys*, that the brigadier turned in dismay to my father, who, with a smile on his face, was watching the disappearing mob from the city. After a short consultation, guns and ammunition were carried into the tower as the brigadier had made up his mind not to abandon it, in hopes that help would be sent, ere long, from Meerut.

But alas! Soon after a puff of white smoke, followed by a magnificent coronal of red dust high above the city walls, told its own tale. The magazine had exploded! The report that followed was drowned by the loud cries of the *sepoys* who rushed to their arms shouting *Deen! Deen!* and there was confusion and dismay. My mother understood the full purport of the words, and resolved to fly from such a treacherous and unreliable support ere it was too late. She told my father it was time, Delhi was left to its fate, and we would fare better in the fields! At that moment, to add to horrors, two carts containing the bodies of the poor Europeans who had been killed that morning were driven up to the tower.

The drivers insolently declared that ere evening our fates would be the same. This settled matters, and though some of the gentlemen tried to overrule their determination (the brigadier going so far as to say my mother was striking a panic) they were firm advising the others to follow their example. We were once more in the carriage flying for our lives through cantonments up the Karnal road (the only one open to us, for all the roads to the city were overrun with enemies).

About four miles out of Delhi stood a small house which belonged to the *nawab* who had come to warn us on the night of the 10th. It stood to the left of the road, in the centre of a mango grove, the tall, thick trees completely hiding it. The *nawab* had often asked my father to visit the place, but we had never availed ourselves of the invitation, now it appealed to us as a quiet shelter and retreat. It was a miserable place, and seemed doubly dreary under the circumstances in which we were placed, but there was a sense of security inside its walls, as my father had on several occasions been of trifling service to the *nawab* for which he seemed grateful. The servants in charge readily admitted us, and promised us succour and help. We had no money and no food, so the coachman was sent back to the bearer to ask for these. My father gave him his signet ring, in case the bearer did not credit that he had been sent to ask for the necessaries.

He went with fair promises but never returned. The *nawab's malee* (gardener) also thought he would go to his master, tell him we were there, and get his orders from him as to whether we were to stay on in the house. Both the servants seemed frightened, and begged my father not to show himself, in case some of the rebels suspecting we were there might follow.

The carriage and horses were led round to the back of the house, and all traces of wheels leading from the gate carefully obliterated. My father and stepsister (Miss Haldane), the latter carrying me in her arms, went up to the top of the house from whence the city could be seen. My mother decided to stay below. Here there was peace and quiet and security at last for we did not think the *nawab* would fail us! And now my mother thought out a plan that would ward off suspicion, in case they came to search for fugitives. The compound was a very large one with an untidy ill-kept garden, with large trees and shrubs overhanging the narrow road leading to the house. It had a high wall right round made of solid masonry, and just the one entrance, which led to the Karnal road. One side, under the trees there was a well, with a low parapet, near this stood the *chowkidar's* hut with a small clearance in front.

My mother felt that at such a time no reliance could be placed in a native, she regretted deeply that the *malee* and coachman had been permitted to go to the city for she felt that these very ones might betray our whereabouts and be the undoing of us; so she determined to keep the *chowkidar* under her eye, especially as he kept on asking her what he should do or say if any of the rebels came to look for us. "For sheltering the *Feringees* they will kill me also!" He kept repeating. She told him not to fear, but to do as she told him, and all would be well.

In front of the hut stood the *chowkidar's* cot, and on this she seated herself, drawing her skirt from the back over her head to look like a *chudder* completely veiling her face as the native women do. Then she made the man light a fire, bring out his cooking pots, and set him to work to cook some bread for she said "We are very hungry, and will eat what you cook for us, and I will pay you well for it."

She told him if any troopers came, he was not to move from that spot, but to tell them that the house was empty, and that they might go over it if they were so minded, and see for themselves that no *Feringees* were concealed there.

The *Sahib* has loaded guns and is watching from the roof *if you betray us, he will shoot you first*, I have only to raise my hand as a signal for him to fire and I will do so without hesitation if you do not obey me, so beware!

The man, between terror of the *Sahib* and his deadly weapons, and the dread of troopers and city *badmashes* was in abject misery, and readily promised to obey! The beautiful moon had risen in all her splendour, and the peace and stillness around contrasted strangely with the sights and sounds of the distant city where in the soft light the lurid glare of many a fire in cantonments, flickering, and blazing above the trees, told its own terrible tale of destruction and death.

Shots could be distinctly heard, and ever and anon the boom of a cannon, while borne on the breeze came the incessant uproar of a raging bloodthirsty multitude, so still and quiet was the spot. What must my poor parents have felt on that awful night, in that isolated garden burdened as they were with a sense of loneliness, a weight of sorrow and anxiety and a dread of horrors to come, with the knowledge that our beautiful home was plundered and burnt, with nowhere to go to without even a change of linen; nor so much as a *rupee* between us! In that dark hour they prayed earnestly for help and guidance and it was given them.

My father was entirely led by my mother's keener insight and better judgment for he knew that she thoroughly understood the native character, and he trusted her steady, determined manner of dealing with them. He knew very little of the language, and had not been out in India long, therefore his clashing at such a time with them would have been utterly fatal to us for being quick-tempered he would never have borne their insolent, high-handed behaviour and most probably have struck them for it. This would have resulted in our all being killed.

My mother had made him promise not to be hasty or lose his

temper, however great the provocation, *and to shoot when only necessary*. Extra wisdom was given her that day, to enable her to show such calm courage and fortitude; and then she had her children to think of. My sister was only fourteen and I, an infant just able to walk. Had my father by a hasty word or act committed himself he would instantly have suffered for it and what would our fate have been!

Twice the rebels came to the gate and hailed the *chowkidar* asking him if he knew where the fugitives from the tower had gone.

The last trooper came to within a few yards of where my mother was seated, reined in his horse and called out in a threatening manner that he had been told Europeans were hidden in the house, and they were to be hunted out forthwith. The man, fearing for his life, obeyed the injunctions given him, and without moving from the spot told the trooper that some Europeans had driven up early in the evening, but he had refused to admit them, and they had driven on towards Karnal. "The house lies open, search the place if you doubt my word," he said.

The prompt reply seemed satisfactory, and the rebel hurried off in search of other victims.

Our fate truly hung in the balance in that awful moment, but the homely sight of the man busy over his cooking, and the woman quietly looking on, with the house in the background, its doors and windows thrown wide open disarmed suspicion and left no room for doubt besides there was much to be done elsewhere! So, the ruse proved a success. It was now nearing midnight and the coachman had not returned, and as no one seemed stirring, my mother thought she would go round to the back and have a look at the horses to see that they were all right. She made the *chowkidar* go with her for she feared to trust him alone.

She found them grazing under the trees where they were tethered but there were no signs of the *syces*. They had absconded. As she turned towards the house, she saw the figure of a native standing near the *chowkidar* talking to him in a low tone. It was the *malee* who had returned from the *nawab* to say that "not the dog belonging to a Christian was to be allowed the shelter of his roof!" He had strict orders to turn us out, and we must go.

He went on to say that the road was infested with rebels and ruffians who were on the lookout, knowing that we were in hiding close by, these might come in at any moment to search the house so it would be better if we went at once, delay would make it more difficult, and by daylight the chance of escape would be remote. So, my poor mother turned to the house, and seeing a ladder propped against the back leading to the roof she climbed this with some difficulty and told my father what the men were saying, and of the *nawab's* treachery and ingratitude. My parents hid us in one of the back rooms.

They gave my sister a loaded pistol to fire at any native who entered for the report of the pistol would bring them back at once and asking God to protect us, they descended the ladder taking the harness with them. The *nawab's* servants were asked to help in harnessing the horses but refused to touch either saying it was a *Chamar* or sweeper's place to do that. This piece of insolence showed that their master's orders had had their effect for hitherto they had been civil and willing enough to do as they were told.

The horses were a fine pair, young and powerful and knew my parents well so there was no difficulty in harnessing them and bringing them on to the road. When my mother had mounted the box, and taken the reins in hand my father fetched us, and placed us in the carriage with all the guns and ammunition and then taking two loaded pistols, he seated himself on the box near my mother. The *chowkidar* was then told to open wide the gates leading out of the compound and to place large stones against them to prevent their closing to. My mother meant to make a dash out of the place, and to let the horses go their best speed till we were clear of it, for she now feared that the rebels were looking about, and only waiting to get us in the open to attack us.

My father had his pistols ready to hand. The guns were all loaded and my sister was prepared to hand these up as they were needed. The treachery and deceit lately shown had so enraged my father that he had determined not to waste a single shot—to aim deliberately and make good use of his weapons. The spirited horses only too delighted to be on the move, started forward with a bound, but my mother who was a splendid "whip" had them well under control; and we were out of the gate in a second, tearing madly up the Grand Trunk Road to Karnal, The night was almost as clear as the day. On either side, as we drove lay the fields and the free open country, straight ahead nothing but the long stretch of white road on which any object might be seen some distance away—so bright was the moonlight—quiet reigned supreme!

My mother drew reins to ease the horses and walk them for a bit. She had no fixed plans, and did not know what was before us. The village people might be friendly, or they too might have turned against us. That remained to be seen, and soon was proved. We could not have gone far, when, in the distance, there seemed to be a crowd of men drawn up across the road. These were evidently after no good so my father prepared for defence. As the carriage approached, they closed in with loud yells, completely blocking the way. My father pointed his gun at the mob and called out *Hut jao!* This had the desired effect, but they followed the carriage, flourishing clubs and sticks in a menacing manner and abusing us. We trotted on and soon put distance between us, but only to fall in with a stronger party.

This time more formidable for they carried spears, *talwars* and *lathis* (iron-bound clubs). They drew a line across the road calling on us to *thamo* (stop)! These were Jats, a well-known tribe of *dacoits*. Their desire was to secure the carriage and horses without injuring them and to dispose of us. My father aimed at the foremost and said "*Hut jao* or I will shoot you." With a yell of fury, they rushed at us, and one more daring than the rest seized the reins. My father seeing threats were useless, fired and the villain fell dead beside the carriage. The reins slipped from his grasp, the horses startled at the report and the wild yells of the savages plunged forward. The rest fell back and we dashed on.

Some of the men tried to overtake us, howling curses and execrations at us, but their swiftest runners could not come up with the maddened horses. One of their number who seemed to be gaining, using foul and abusive language to my parents as he ran was also shot dead. When they were out of sight and hearing my mother slackened speed to ease the horses. She spoke soothing, reassuring words to them, for they were now very nervous and restive and started at the least sound or shadow across the road, her voice calmed them and after some time they steadied down and walked. This gave my father time to reload his weapons, and examine the harness to see that it was all right.

The Jats and Gujars have a peculiar war cry, weird and wild like the jackal which travels far, and means much to those who know the tribe. This "call" with a plaintive wail in it seemed now to come from several directions. Loud and menacing as we advanced and taken up, and echoed faintly in the rear (where they were deploring the fate of two of their party). Evidently, they were gathering and concentrating forces ahead, while those we had left behind were crying on their brethren to avenge their dead!

My mother explained *this* to my father preparing him for another struggle. The horses were allowed their heads, while my parents braced themselves for the encounter, telling my sister to sit well back under the hood of the carriage (which was up) and to be ready with the guns. To my mother's reassuring words "Don't be afraid" she replied "Not I!" so bravely and cheerfully that it nerved my parents for the encounter, while I slept peacefully in her arms! The lot we *now* saw seemed determined to have our lives, for they rushed forward yelling their loudest, and so terrified the poor horses by their savage onslaught that it needed all my mother's strength and good handling to keep them from swerving and running off the road into the *kutcha* dinted hollows on either side.

They swarmed round us in a second, hitting wildly with their *talwars* and clubs. My father knocked over their leader but, nothing daunted, the rest beset us on all sides. As we tore past one of them hit my poor mother a tremendous blow with a *lathi* on the right arm, but she never uttered a sound for fear it would upset my father. The villain was shot dead. At the same time, one ran along with the carriage and made a cut with his *talwar* at my father. My sister, well on the alert, called out "Look to your left!" and this ruffian too was knocked over before he could do harm. One desperate wretch climbed the hood and was in the act of striking a blow which would have killed one of my parents, but a pistol bullet in the forehead sent him tumbling backwards. The sword just grazed my father on the nape of the neck and fell clattering at my sister's feet! Once more beaten, and discomfited, with a loss of four or five of their number, we got through them, but they continued the phase, hurling spears and large stones at the rear as long as they were able to keep up. We now met a party of the 38th Light Infantry returning from a musketry depot at Amballa.

These shouted at us not to proceed, but feeling that they were more to be dreaded than the villagers, we drove furiously past them and now came our most desperate fight for life, for we went headlong into a band of Gujars (who were lying in ambush on the sides of the road) and sprang up to meet us. The horses were now mad with terror and rough usage, and my poor mother, with her arm almost helpless from the blow she had received, felt that another encounter with these wretches would prove disastrous. In that terrible moment she lost heart and hope for the first time and chose the "lesser evil of the two." She felt that if the *sepoys* did not protect us, they would shoot us, and it would soon be over, so on their mercy she meant to rely.

In an instant she had turned the carriage and was driving back at full speed. When the *sepoys* heard the ramble of wheels, they moved their wagons off the centre of the road and stood awaiting us. The *havildar* (native officer) of the party came forward to meet us and addressed my parents very civilly (which was surprising under the circumstances). He seemed (or pretended) to be in ignorance of what had occurred at Delhi and Meerut, and asked where they were going, and "how we came to be so far from our home at that hour of the night?" My mother explained matters, told him we were fugitives, and in great distress begging of him to protect us from the Gujars who had followed us, and stood looking on.

At a word from the *havildar* the *sepoys* surrounded the carriage, telling the Gujars to keep clear, and threatening to shoot any who dared to touch us. The moon was full and bright and showed the men's faces clearly. They seemed earnest and kindly disposed. One of them placed his hand on my head and, remarked that it was "pitiful to see so small a child homeless and exposed to such dangers" promising to protect us. The Gujars seeing this seemed inclined to disperse, but the Jats we had fought our way through had also come up, and their leader (a tall powerful man) called the *havildar* aside and said something to him in a whisper. Whatever it was, turned the tide completely, for the *sepoys* were called off and told not to interfere.

My mother was overcome with horror and dismay at the sudden reverse, and the terrible doom that seemed inevitable, surrounded as we were by foes. She entreated the *sepoys* in piteous tones to save us, telling them how these men had attacked us, and beset us in such a determined manner that we had fought through them in sheer desperation, but though they felt the force of her words, and praised my father's pluck, saying he had fired "straight and sure, and was a brave man to have done so, and to have come unscathed through it," they declared they would (or could) not stand by us; for the Jats had a grievance, and were terribly incensed against him, and *were determined to have his life for the ones he had taken.*

My mother made one more attempt to keep them true and loyal to their allegiance. She told them if they valued their honour to return with us to Karnal, and shun Delhi "for retribution is sure to follow this day's evil deeds." The savages had now become impatient (emboldened by their numbers) and called out that if the *sepoys* did not move on, they would attack us in their midst. Then seeing how helpless we were my mother entreated the *sepoys* to put an end to us mercifully by shooting us.

"As Sikander's daughter I am entitled to the protection of all true soldiers, and I claim an honourable death at the hands of soldiers and it will not be to your credit as brave men that you stood by and saw us beaten to death by such cowardly ruffians as these"—pointing with her whip at the mob.

The *sepoys* were completely taken aback at her daring request, and also to hear that she was the daughter of Colonel Skinner. A murmur went round which boded no good to the savages, and the *havildar* spoke: "Ah! you are the brave daughter of a great man, therefore you speak well! We knew the Colonel *Sahib* and it was our regiment which was sent to escort his remains from Rohtak to Delhi, where he is buried."

"If that be so, help us now. As Sikander's daughter I demand your aid or, if you will not protect us, then, at least give us the death we seek," she entreated.

"No, that is impossible," said the *havildar*. "We cannot protect you, nor can we have your blood on our hands; you and your brave *Sahib* go your way. The God who has brought you so far will nerve his arm to shield you, and give you His protection still."

Then turning to the mob, he addressed them saying that the *Sahib* had only fired in self-defence, and if his aim was true it was *kismet*, and while we were in sight none should molest us, for they would not look on unmoved at our deaths.

So, we had to make a desperate rush through the enemy once more. As we did so a few shots were fired, but as they did us no harm, I conclude the *sepoys* let off their muskets to intimidate the savages who followed us with blood curdling yells, and soon swarmed round us. My father stood up to make better use of his firearms. My mother urged the horses on, but they crowded round striking the horses now in their mad fury, as well as at my parents on the box. A few yards ahead was a bridge, with a low parapet on either side. As we drove over this, down went the horses over some obstacle which could not be seen. My mother (as I have said before) was a splendid whip. She rallied the poor creatures and pulled them up sharp, and dashed on again, but the check had brought our foes upon us in numbers and they were trying to knock the horses on the heads; so, my father fired rapidly and shot a few, and we got through once more.

The horses were now showing signs of fatigue and had to be urged with whip and voice; moreover, a peculiar grating sound seemed to come from one of the wheels which showed that the carriage had sustained some injury. As soon as the "coast was clear" my father got down to see what was wrong, and was horrified to find that one of the wheels had been cut half through by the iron step of the coach box, which had bent back to such an extent that it had eaten into all the spokes of the left fore-wheel. Evidently, they had tied a rope across the bridge to impede our progress, but it had given way. He managed to knock it into its place with the butt end of his pistol (which broke in the attempt) and stones. In this encounter my father received a blow on the arm, one of the pistols was smashed, and one of the gun barrels injured by a blow from a *lathi*. The horses had cuts and bruises all over.

The carriage bore marks of ill-usage for many a day, but thank God, our foes were now thoroughly discouraged, and made no attempts to follow us, nor were we molested at close quarters again, the cowards confining their attacks to throwing stones at us from behind bridges, which providentially struck none of us, though two or three found their way into the carriage. They had lost a number and been taught a lesson they were not likely to forget, and as their villages were not far apart, no doubt they found the means to warn those ahead that the *Sahib* was well armed, and could use his weapons to some purpose, as they had found to their cost. Dawn was just breaking when we reached a small *chowki*. At this we stopped and asked for the *chowkidar*.

A man standing in the doorway answered in an offhand tone "There is none."

"There must be," said my mother "and the sooner he presents himself the better, for we intend taking shelter here."

The fellow laughed and said "Who are we to be responsible to? The reign of the *Feringees* is over, and we are free to do as we please."

"Is it?" said my mother. "This day the British foot is planted firmer in India than it ever was before." She told him "for a short time they might triumph and please themselves, but English vengeance would surely overtake them, and *for every drop of English blood that was shed they would be made to pay back tenfold.*"

The Asiatic is a craven at heart, and her bold words and the assurance with which they were uttered took him aback completely; he slunk off to do her bidding without another word. The horses were taken out of the carriage, and led to a well close by. My parents gave them a drink and dashed water all over them to refresh them. The poor creatures were fagged and beat, and behaved like lambs. Then, finding that the natives about (though they held aloof, and looked askance) showed no signs of animosity, for the first time they thought of their own hurts and injuries, and attended to them. My poor mother's arm was a sight. It was swollen to such an extent that the sleeve had to be ripped up from wrist to shoulder. On the dark contusion were livid marks showing the iron ring bands of the *lathi* distinctly where the full force of the blow had fallen.

She told my father that when she felt the blow, she thought she had been shot, but feared to let him know thinking it would upset him. So, she had borne it in patience, though she was sick and giddy and faint with pain till we were out of danger. She tore strips from her petticoat, my father wet these and bound up the arm. While this was being done, some harmless looking villagers (unarmed) had gathered out of curiosity near the well, and were looking on. One, a wizened up old man with caste marks in the forehead, seemed much concerned, and kept on asking my mother how she came to be so badly hurt, and plying her with questions as to the bloodstains on my father's coat, and the bruised and battered state of the horses and carriage—questions which passed unheeded for no native now appeared trustworthy but he persisted, and went on to explain that he was a Brahmin and of great importance in the village and "Brahmins were not a bloodthirsty race, and never took life. If we trusted him, he would save us."

Although this fellow and those with him seemed disposed to assist, as their appearance was not prepossessing and my parents could not avoid a doubt as to their intentions, however, they thought anywhere off the road would be safer as it was now daylight, so my mother asked him what he purposed doing. He pointed at the village which was some distance from the well and said "my home is there, if you come with me, I will give you food and shelter till nightfall; and then you can go your way."

He assured us that under his roof we would be safe. "A Brahmin is never false to his word."

We were in sad need of food and rest and *any refuge in a storm*, so we went. The horses were harnessed to the carriage, but as the road was a *kutcha* cart track, the horses were led by my mother; my father walked beside her, carrying two loaded guns; the Brahmin and his party a little in advance. As we neared the village two youths came towards us, looked knowingly at the Brahmin and enquired whither he was leading us. The old villain pointed ahead, upon which they laughed, and one called out "give them comfortable *charpais* to rest on and may their sleep be sound and long."

My mother understood the taunt and all it meant. These fiends were going to poison us.

"Turn back, there is treachery here," she exclaimed, and my father had to do what she thought best, though the words only expressed a kindly solicitude for our ease and comfort and welfare as far as he could gather. We returned to the *chowki* and found two new arrivals there. One (a respectable looking fellow with a flowing white beard) seemed to know my mother, though she had no recollection of him. He *salaamed* low, and taking off his turban, laid it at her feet. "You are one of Sikander *Sahib's* daughters," he remarked.

This mark of extreme respect coming at such a time was astonishing especially as she noticed that the man was of some importance from the deferential manner of the other natives present, towards him.

"Who are you?" she enquired.

"I have eaten the Colonel *Sahib's* salt for many years, and I will give my life for any of his children," the old man replied.

My mother was uncertain how to act, and hesitated.

"How can I depend upon you, and be sure you are not as false as the rest in this hot bed of deceit and sedition? We have just escaped one trap laid for our lives."

"Those," he replied, pointing to the Brahmin and his friends, "had taken you prisoners and meant to kill you, but you can trust me, I will not betray the salt I have been nurtured on, but you must do as I advise and leave the rest to me. This is an evil day for the *Feringees* and the natives are most incensed against the *Sahiblog*. Therefore, you must put the *Sahib* into the carriage whilst you drive; I will sit beside you on the box. Tell the *Sahib* not to speak and do not object to raise your hand in token of recognition of the obeisance that is made to you by the natives, who pass us and *salaam*. We shall meet many, and it will cost you nothing to touch your forehead each time in acknowledgment of the respect they show you."

This plan seemed simple enough, so my father took his seat in the carriage. The old fellow mounted the box, and his *bhai* (the other man who he said was his brother) sat behind in the syce's place. The sun was high in the heavens when we left the *chowki* and its power was beginning to be felt. My mother soaked a cloth and bound it round her head for it was aching cruelly, and she could hardly keep her eyes open. So, another day of weary journeying before us, and no certainty how it would end, or what the night would bring. The horses were allowed to take it easy, for they had been without food all the time. At every well they were given a drink, and cold water was splashed over them to refresh them.

The old fellow was very talkative, and now told my mother that he was *Zemindar* (headman of one of my grandfather's villages—an old and trusty retainer who had known my mother and all Colonel

Skinner's children since their babyhood, had watched them grow up, and only lost sight of my mother when she married Captain Haldane and left her father's home at Hansi to go with his regiment to Neemuch. All this happened years before. Captain Haldane was killed at Chillianwalla (Sikh War) and my mother had married my father.

The old home and its associations forgotten long since by her, were yet fresh in his memory, and a glance at her face had been enough to recall them. As she drove, the faithful old fellow rambled on bringing to her mind many an incident of those early days, many a childish exploit and deed of mischief which quite convinced her that he really was what he professed to be (an old servant of the family) and she felt she had found a *friend*, and need have no further fears for our safety.

It was most providential we met him, for now there was a marked difference in the manner of all the village people we passed. They stared at first, then made a low *salaam*, raising both hands to their foreheads; and my mother did not forget to acknowledge the salute. Some of these villagers told us that not far ahead were several other *Sahibs* and if we drove fast, we would overtake them. We did, and true enough, there were the friends we had left behind at the tower and never hoped to see again. The party consisted of Brigadier Graves, Mr. LeBas, Captain Nicoll, Lieutenants Grant, Taylor, Mew, Martineau, Drummond and the Sergeant-Major of the 74th Native Infantry—a strong party and well-armed. Of the rest they could give no news. All had fled from the tower shortly after we left to seek safety elsewhere.

I was forgetting to mention that just before we left the tower our old baker who supplied the station with bread, ran breathlessly up to the door, and presented the whole basket to my mother. The loaves were distributed among the ladies who were in the tower, but in the confusion, we did not take our share, and we had now been 24 hours without food, exposed to the hot sun and hotter blast. Mr. LeBas was quite upset when he saw the terrible havoc the last few hours had worked on the faces of my mother and sister. Suffering so patiently borne, terror and anxiety so bravely overcome lest it should have a demoralising effect on my father who had to fight for us all. He remembered that he had a crust of bread in one of his pockets, and produced it after a search. This was given to me for I was very hungry and kept on crying for food.

Those who have experienced an Indian summer and been out in the months of May and June will perhaps realise what we went through on that awful day, used as we were to every luxury and comfort. About 4 p.m. we reached Panipat. Shortly after we arrived the *tahsildar* of the place came over to pay his respects to my parents and see if he could be of any use. Our old friend the *zemindar* had told him of our hard fight for life the night before and how he had found us. Colonel Skinner's name was well known here as most of the villages belonged to him and are still in the Skinner estate. We drove to the *Tahsil* and ordered some food and milk, also a feed for the poor horses, and having rested for a while resumed the journey to Karnal reinforced by *sowars* from the *Kotwali*. The *tahsildar* himself accompanied us part of the way.

On the morning of the 13th we reached Karnal, and drove straight to the house of the Judge (Mr. McWhirter) who had invited us to spend some time there before the outbreak. On enquiries we were told the master was still in Delhi. As we never heard of him again it is certain he was killed. What a treat the comfortable well-kept house must have been! Here all was quiet, servants civil and willing to wait on us. So worn out and weary were we that we threw ourselves on the beds and were soon fast asleep—all but my mother who shortly roused us to drink some tea she had made which was most refreshing.

The rest of our party (who had gone at first to the *dâk* bungalow) also came over to the house, so we were now a good number—ten men and two ladies. British troops were expected daily from Amballa, so feeling pretty secure the gentlemen resolved to stay on at Karnal. But all manner of evil tidings poured in from the neighbouring district, so much so that it became a question for serious consideration whether we should be safe for any time. There were panics daily which kept the men on the alert night and day. With no change of clothes, it is a wonder how we managed to look clean. The food was good under my mother's careful management and supervision, for which we were very thankful. The Nawab of Karnal was said to be friendly and used to come and sit with the gentlemen every evening.

After a few days Doctor Balfour and his sister-in-law (Miss Smith), Mr. Thompson (Engineer) and Mrs. Trouson joined us. They had had a terrible journey, having escaped on a gun-carriage, riding all day and travelling at night. Mrs. Trouson had gone through much sorrow and suffering. She and her sister (who was also married) were trying to escape at the Cashmere gate, when the latter, with her baby in her arms, was shot down. The infant was unhurt, but the poor mother wounded severely. In her agony she entreated Mrs. Trouson to save her baby and to run for her life, for she was past help. Mrs. Trouson took the unfortunate little one and escaped. She tried to keep it alive on biscuits and water, but it died for want of proper nourishment on the way. She was lifted out of the gun-carriage, and it was discovered that two of her ribs and collar bone were broken.

Miss Smith was so bruised and disfigured that she was barely recognisable. So different to the pretty, light-hearted English girl we had parted with only a few days before! What a chapter of horrors had intervened! News was now received that two squadrons of the 4th Light Cavalry had been sent from Amballa to guard the Treasury at Thanesar (near Karnal) as the 4th, together with the 5th and 60th Native Infantry were reported disaffected, to use no stronger term the proximity of these native troops with the temptation of a treasury to plunder did not improve our condition, as it was feared they might first rob the treasury and then come down on Karnal. The only guard we had was some 30 or 40 *sepoys* of the 60th Native Infantry and it was reasonably agreed that they might follow the example of their comrades at Amballa and rush into open mutiny at any moment. The gentlemen were prepared for the worst, slept with pistols under their pillows, "one eye open" and guns handy. The compound was patrolled by *chowkidars* provided by the Deputy Collector of Karnal (who took endless delight in letting out unearthly sounds and cries at odd hours of the night to show they were on the *qui vive*) and some *sowars* furnished by the Nawab of Karnal, but little faith was placed in these so-called protectors.

One morning there was great excitement, for there appeared in our midst a young man who had ridden all the way from Amballa across country to open the telegraph line between Karnal and that station. My father found him at dawn seated on the veranda steps too dead beat to move. He made over a formidable brace of pistols (which he said had done good service on the way) to my father to keep, while he proceeded with his work. At 9 a. m. the office was open and the *first message despatched was a request that some intelligence regarding the army intended for Delhi might be forwarded.* The reply was that all was *en train* and that His Excellency would command in person. The same evening a letter came from Captain MacAndrew stating that he was close at hand with a force of artillery, cavalry, and infantry belonging to the Patiala and Jhind *Rajas* who had sent in their allegiance to the British Government.

On the 17th this force, to our relief, marched in; for although no great faith could be placed in their loyalty, still it was something to know that a number of armed men had accompanied a British officer so far without injuring him and that was of itself a sort of guarantee for their good behaviour. Meanwhile the country about was in a very disturbed state. Villages might be seen blazing at night, old feuds between rival *zemindars* were made a pretext for murder, plunder, cattle raids, and all sorts of villainy. The acting magistrate, Mr. Richards did all he could to check crime, and uphold his authority, but it was a difficult task. On the night of the 17th welcome intelligence reached us that a small force of Europeans, consisting of about 500 men of all arms, was to leave Amballa for Karnal immediately.

This force was sent in consequence of an earnest requisition from Mr, LeBas to the commander-in-chief for the purpose of awing the people of Karnal who had begun to discredit the report about the march of the British soldiers from Amballa, Mr. LeBas concluded his message with the intimation that if European troops were not immediately pushed on, he should at once leave Karnal, with the party of Delhi fugitives under his care—a move that would have left the place in the enemy's hands, and the Treasury and city would have been attacked and plundered. That night, about eleven, Major Nicoll raised the alarm that we were about to be attacked. The gentlemen promptly turned out with their weapons, the ladies assisting in carrying spare guns and ammunition and placing them to hand and in various ways rendering themselves useful. For about an hour the men remained under arms, when it was found to be nothing worse than a trifling disturbance in the city.

The *sowars* hearing the noise had let off their matchlocks to create a panic, and no doubt to test the mettle of the *Sahibs*. Sleep that night was out of the question. Every two or three hours a telegram arrived from Amballa or a letter from the neighbourhood, with news the nature of which was generally read in the countenances of those who perused the contents. From the north rumours of mutiny and the Meerut massacre was beginning to get abroad. All communication below was cut off, and when a stray letter arrived it gave little to hope for. From the stations beyond Meerut there was no sign! Simla was said to be in jeopardy owing to the disaffection of the Ghurkas stationed at Jutog, and much anxiety was manifested about the large number of ladies and children up there.

Rumour had it that the whole country was up in arms against the white folk and nothing short of their extermination would settle matters. Meanwhile everything was done to allay the alarm, and to make the best of what was a very bad state of affairs. Doctor Stewart was appointed Postmaster, and every exertion was made to open communication with Meerut and Saharunpur. The drivers of mail carts were handsomely rewarded for information, and something quite extravagant was promised to the first man who should bring news of the proximity of the long looked for European force.

At last they came—on the night of the 18th. They remained in barracks all next day, but owing to a rumour that a number of the 4th Cavalry were in the neighbourhood, a full company of the 1st E. B. Fusiliers, under Lieutenant Owen, was ordered into the compound that night, and having piled arms, lay about the steps and ground in delightful confusion. Few will ever forget the feeling of security which that night pervaded the house. The ladies greeted the young officer as if he had been an old friend instead of one they had never seen before, and had they been possessed of any money they would gladly have given it all among the soldiers—so full of gratitude were their hearts that night, and for the first time since they left Delhi—one and all slept soundly with a guard of British soldiers at the door.

Soon after this a *shigram* (cart) arrived bringing Doctor Wood and Captain Peile (the former badly wounded in the face with a musket ball), Mrs. Peile and Mrs. Wood.

On the 21st Captain Hodson started with 400 *sowars* to clear the way to Meerut. On the same day Captain MacAndrew proceeded towards Panipat for the same purpose, with some guns and Irregular Horse, and that afternoon Captain Sandford came in with 25 loyal troopers of the 3rd Cavalry, with despatches for the chief, having come *via* Baghpat and across country. He started off for Amballa by mail cart leaving the troopers picketed in the compound. Mutinous *sepoys* were continually captured and brought in by the British troops, but they were always released and allowed to go their way, which was of course to swell the lists at Delhi!

One afternoon a meek looking *chaprasie* belonging to Mr. Richards was heard to say "If I only had a *talwar* the first head I severed would be my master's!" but being a Brahmin such a murderous desire did not count, so a cocked pistol was placed at his own, and after a good scaring he was allowed to go to his home! It was not thought good policy to execute summary justice, hence the mistake! Soon after this the chief arrived, but his visit was not of long duration, as he died suddenly after a dinner party given in his honour. It was now decided to make arrangements to convey the ladies to Amballa and thence to

41

Simla. A day or two later the party under my father's care started off in *doolies*. After weary days of trouble and annoyance Parker's hotel was reached in safety; here we spent a night and proceeded to Kalka.

As we moved out of the compound at Amballa, a friend warned my father of some expected outbreak on the parade ground, where the 5th Native Infantry were being disarmed. My father got out and walked beside our *doolies* until we were clear of Amballa. There was a great shouting as we crossed the parade, and the *kahars* (*doolie*- bearers) remarked on it, but nothing occurred and we went safely on till we got to Kalka. At daybreak the splendid scenery of the Himalayas is a sight to behold! The peace and repose prevailing contrasted strangely with the fearful scenes so recently witnessed and gone through, and soon we were out of the hot blast of the plains in the pretty station of Kasauli, with the pleasing sight of European sentries pacing in front of the barracks, and the women and children sitting in the verandas to all appearance as happy and joyous as if the barbarities of the 11th May had never been perpetrated. The barracks were in a state of defence; the doors and windows double planked with loop holes at them all, in readiness in case of an attack. The jaunty, careless air of the British soldier was very comforting. After a short stay at the *dâk* bungalow, my father forwarded a letter from the late General Hallifax to the officer commanding at Kasauli, for permission to occupy quarters in the barracks, and the reply being favourable, we went.

There were some soldiers on the ground floor below us. These jovial souls were enjoying their evening meal and singing by turns, all joining in the chorus, and finishing off with "Rule Britannia." It was cheering to hear them, and pleasant to see the barrack square lighted up by the full moon rising over the distant hills, but we were worn and weary after our long journey, and needed rest and quiet which we could not get at the barracks, so we went back again to the *dâk* bungalow. Officers who were on leave in the interior and had now heard of the outbreak in the plains, were hastening down to join their regiments, among them several officers of the 9th Lancers who were shooting near the snows, when the tidings reached them. They arrived in an incredibly short time, having ridden day and night, their bronzed countenances bearing unmistakable signs of the exposure they had suffered. Of these fine fellows two fell during the siege.

Every day some fresh arrival made his appearance, all intent upon joining the "Army of retribution." In some cases, their anxiety to hurry on was so great that they did not even set foot in the bungalow, but took a hasty drink and crust of bread or biscuit on horse-back and pursued their journey down to the plains at a break-neck pace. From some of these we learnt that the people at Simla were in a constant state of alarm, partly on account of the groundless rumours spread by unnerved men, some of whom so completely lost their heads as to be wholly unable to control their feelings. One great panic led nearly the whole of Simla to desert their homes and rush—some to conceal themselves in the *khuds* (precipice), some to the Simla Bank, others to the protection of the Keonthal *Rajah*.

A party of these poor creatures (ladies and children) went off with just the clothes to their backs, down the *khuds* and hid in a cave, till, out of hunger and thirst, they tried to get back, but lost their way, and wandered away from their homes, running fearful risks, and meeting with many adventures in their wanderings. They were discovered (nearly distraught and in a pitiful condition) by a gentleman who was out shooting, and conducted safely to their homes which were just as they had left them, nothing missing or stolen. Those who succeeded in reaching Keonthal were sheltered by the *Rajah* in cowsheds. Here they stayed till all danger was over.

The Nussuree Battalion (Gurkhas) having got what they wanted, were pacified, and soon after consented to march to the plains!

Many persons have thought fit to denominate the Simla panics as groundless; but that there was cause for alarm is fully proved by the fact that the Kasauli detachment of the Gurkhas robbed the treasury at that station, burnt a portion of the Chiefs camp equipage at Haripur (near Simla), and after attempting to fire the *dâk* bungalow there were marched into Simla. At the same time, it was known that the Gurkhas stationed at Jutog (Simla) actually refused to march to the plains, defied control and declared that General Anson was concealed, not daring to face the *sepoys*, and they would drag him out and murder him! But by the merciful interposition of Providence, their hands were stayed, and after some delay they gave in. This was the great Simla panic of 1857; but there were others owing to the frequent rumours rising in the *bazaar* and spreading like wild fire from house to house.

Muhammadan servants were known to threaten the defenceless and helpless ladies whose husbands were fighting the government cause in the plains, and to scare little children by telling them of the fearful tortures they would inflict on them ere long. They were short and curt in their answers to their masters, and strutted about as if they were not serving at all, but merely working to please themselves. One of these vermin hinted that he was not our servant, and should therefore do as he liked about bringing our food, clean or dirty, hot or cold!

When the news became more cheering, their chap-fallen faces reflected it, which showed that they too had sources of information, and as matters began to mend, they rapidly descended to their former state of abject servility, and would have grovelled at our feet and kissed them had they been permitted to do so!

With not a single British soldier in the place, and officers ordered down, things looked gloomy enough. A small Volunteer Corps was organised and drilled daily by a non-commissioned officer and inspected by an officer of Her Majesty's Service. To this plucky band of Europeans, and the excellent measures adopted by the Superintendent of the Hill States (Lord William Hajes) Simla owes its freedom from any participation in the Mutiny of 1857. On the occasion of the Eed festival the Muhammadans assembled in great numbers at their meeting place in the bazaar, and were apparently very much excited and disturbed. So much so that it was feared they meant to give trouble, but it was so arranged that at the same hour (when their zeal was at its height) the small band of Volunteers with muskets and row of glistening bayonets should be at their drill on the church *maidan* just above.

The proximity of these and the preparations made for their reception were not altogether pleasing to the Mussulmans for they dispersed without further ado.

Meanwhile officers, sick and wounded, were daily arriving from the plains. None brought good news, and many who would have told a dismal tale, held their peace. To such a pitiful state had matters arrived that the report of a gun fired by some hill *shikari* startled the strongest nerves.

"When things are at the worst they mend." At last came the joyful intelligence "Delhi has fallen." The city was taken and the rebels had been well punished.

We were then living in a house at Simla belonging to Captain Pengree, which he lent us. During the time we were at Kasauli my father continued the *Delhi Gazette* and called it the *Delhi Gazette* extra. He was helped by some reliable friends in authority at Simla with news, and the Lawrence Asylum Press printed the slips which were then distributed. We had no money and were often put to great straits, till two friends who had escaped from the plains joined us and shared the house, and our combined means helped us to live till my father found some work.

How often, during that time of misfortune, my mother regretted that she had not listened to our old *ayah* and hidden some of her valuable jewellery about her before we left our home!

The *ayah* had brought her the case full of costly ornaments, and suggested that she should string some of the most valuable rings round her waist (under the skirt), but she had turned in anger upon the woman, and told her to be gone out of her sight with the box. She feared the *ayah* would talk, and our lives would be doubly in jeopardy if it became known that we had these things with us. The box and its contents were never heard of again!

We escaped with just the clothes to our backs, and a few trinkets my mother and sister were wearing such as brooches, rings, etc., which were not worth much. My father gave his gold watch and chain out of gratitude to the old *zemindar* at Panipat, and his signet ring was given to the coachman at the *nawab's* house, so there was nothing that could be turned into money to buy us the bare necessaries of life. We were beggared and living on the charity of our friends!

Sometime after the siege when it was safe to travel, and the roads had been cleared of the rebels and city *budmashes* who had been driven from Delhi, we travelled down to the plains—first to Amballa, where we made a short stay, then on to Delhi.

My father often spoke of that entry into the great city we had fled from in terror a few short months before.

We entered by the Lahore gate, at which there was now a strong guard of British soldiers. Near the gate we were joined by a small party of officers on horse-back (general and staff). As these passed through, the old officer drew rein, raised his helmet and exclaimed, "All honour to you brave men!" and passed through with the rest.

Our carriage being last my father pulled up, and said a few kind words to the men in praise and recognition of their valour (which seemed to please them) and was about to drive on when one of the soldiers pointed solemnly upwards. My mother and sister glanced quickly up and were horrified to see a *pandy* (rebel *sepoy*) swinging by the neck above their heads, his boots dangling within a few inches of their faces! It gave them a terrible shock, but the soldier explained that there was no cause for alarm since the *pandy* was not a real one but just a figure made up of bamboo and straw, decked out in the uniform they had so lately worn, dishonoured and discarded when they fled in haste from the vengeance at their heels, stripping themselves of their uniforms and accoutrements and flinging them helter-skelter in the streets in their mad desire to get rid of them and escape! For their short triumph was over. Their vain boastings had brought nothing but defeat and disaster, and to be now caught in that guise would mean instant death!

The British Flag was once more hoisted, and the tramp of the British soldier echoed through every street in the great city bringing comfort and assurance to many, and terror and dismay to the rebels and traitors of which there were many still at large skulking about the lanes and byways.

But alas! Our beautiful homes. Nothing but the burnt and charred remains of these were visible. All that was dear to us had perished or was scattered far and wide.

My father took a good sized native *havilee* (house) near the Jumma Musjid, had it thoroughly cleaned and whitewashed, and here we had to make shift for the time being. No amount of plastering or white-washing, however, would obliterate certain ugly looking stains and splashes on the walls which would assert themselves in spite of the coatings of wash laid on. The place was full of horrors, and had an uncanny feel about it, and the nights passed in it were restless and dis-turbed and we were thoroughly uncomfortable and miserable there; but we had to live somewhere, as my father was anxious to start the *Delhi Gazette* Press again and set it going. Many difficulties and ob-stacles stood in the way. First it was hard to find competent workmen for the business, for the old hands were afraid to return to the city, and new ones were not to be relied upon. Perseverance brought its reward.

In time, not only the manager, but some of the others found us out, as also some of our old servants. These had terrible tales to tell of what followed after we left—how the dreaded troopers had ridden up with reeking *talwars* (the city mob at their heels) and demanded the *Feringees* or their own lives in forfeit if they dared to conceal us, till in terror they had fled for their lives! The troopers then sent in some of the *budmashes* to "hunt the dogs out and they would show them some sport." The wretches were only too ready, and rushed in to do their bidding, but finding the place empty they set to work to loot and then fire it. All that they thought valuable they kept, the rest was destroyed!

This is what the old bearer tried to make us believe. Whether the servants had a hand in the disposal and removal of our goods and chat-tels we never found out—nor did we recover a thing (except our old family Bible, which was found during the siege by an artillery officer, embedded in a rubbish heap in the Kudsia Garden. This was restored to us months later, very much discoloured and dirty but intact).

What became of our valuable horses remained a mystery. They were never traced though every effort was made, and a handsome reward offered to anyone who would bring them back. The good creatures that took us so bravely to Karnal (doing the distance from Delhi to Panipat without food or rest in less than 12 hours) on the terrible night of the 11th May, were left with Mr. LeBas at Karnal, who sent them to us (with the carriage) after the siege.

We were glad to welcome them and they were made much of to their dying days. It had got abroad that we had all been killed on the night of the 11th, Two of my stepsisters were at school at the Mussoorie Convent. The good nuns believed the report, and broke the news as kindly as they could to the poor girls who were old enough to realise what it meant, and took it keenly to heart. Upon this followed days of terror and uncertainty, for Mussoorie had its full share of panics and alarms, though all that was possible was put into execution to suppress the cruel (and often idle) tales that were spread from house to house, which mostly originated in the *bazaar.*

One morning a report prevailed that the Gurkhas had mutinied at Dehra and were hurrying up hill to attack the residents at Mussoorie. This led to a general stampede of the whole school! The poor girls frantic like frightened sheep, not caring where they went, and stumbling in their frenzy and despair, scattered far and wide down the steep *khuds* and were with difficulty got together again by two determined nuns. These, though quite as nervous and alarmed, took pains to control their feelings sufficiently to enable them to calm, reassure and instil a sense of discipline into a few of the older girls, who then helped them to search for and collect the flock! Some of the little ones were found hidden in a cave, badly hurt and bleeding, their clothes in rags, and wild terror in their eyes!

After this the lady superior of the Convent wrote to the Officer in charge of the Station and begged him to protect the school from these alarms, with the result that some of the bigger boys at Haddock's School (close by) were provided with ponies, guns and ammunition.

Thus armed, ready for the fray, and enjoying themselves immensely they sallied forth to guard and patrol the station! Their cheery call "All's Well!" now loud and clear, taken up further away, and echoed faintly in the distance in the stillness of the night (at all hours) showing that they were on the alert, and the poor terror-stricken inhabitants might rest in security.

What if a sudden clatter of hoofs on the planked veranda or gravel outside, startled some sleeper into a sense of the troubled state of affairs. The very sound brought comfort, and the assurance that they were being well looked after, and with a feeling of thankfulness they turned over and slept as they had not slept for nights, with the "boy patrols" outside!

One of my stepsisters fared badly in this scare. She fell down the *khud* and was terribly shaken and cut, and bruised so much so that when she came to us at Christmas she was still showing signs of the effect it had had upon her nervous system. She used to waken from profound sleep to scream that the natives were trying to kill her, and beg my sisters to hide her. Always a gentle timid child, that shock proved too much for her. She told us of a fright she had received before the day of the panic.

She had been sent to fetch something from the dining room, and found one of the *khitmatgars* (waiter) laying the table for dinner. When the cruel wretch saw her, he held up a carving knife in a threatening manner and remarked "See! little Miss *baba*, soon you shall be chopped up with *this* to feed the crows. The crows will feed on school misses and grow fat!"

She fled in terror and told the nuns who immediately dismissed the man instead of sending him up for punishment.

Incidents like the above were daily occurrences. Wherever there were defenceless, helpless women and children there were always heartless wretches who took advantage of them, and delighted in torturing them to their utmost ability.

On the other hand, there were a few who helped English ladies and children to escape, or gave them shelter till all danger was past. All these were well rewarded after the mutiny.

The old *zemindar* who befriended us at Panipat, and came to our rescue, was offered a reward of *Rs.* 500 which he refused, saying a good certificate would be more useful. This my father gave him willingly and he went off quite pleased. A month later he came to us in great distress to beg my father to intercede for his two sons who were in the Meerut prison, and had escaped from there on the 10th May, only to be recaptured and sent back to prison. My father who had great influence with the authorities, gladly helped him and secured the freedom of the two youths in return for the good service rendered us by their father though their offence was a serious one, bordering on treason, which meant death in those days.

Parties of natives, suspected of having taken part in the massacre of

Europeans, were brought daily into Delhi and after a brief examination led off and hanged. Amongst the number a young Jat was one day led forth, his chest one mass of sores from a shot wound. My father could not help wondering whether he was one of our murderous assailants on the night of the 11th May, for two of his guns were small shot ones, and the shot scattering would have made just such a wound.

The *nawab* (of Loharoo) who behaved so treacherously to us on the night of the 11th May was for some time in disgrace with the government, who had heard of his disloyalty. His words "not a dog belonging to a Christian should shelter under his roof" had put the noose about his neck, and had my father been in the least vindictive *Nawab Sahib* would have shared the fate of the other traitors who went to their doom! But he pleaded and begged my father's mercy, and asked him to intercede for him, saying it was all a fabrication, and his servant had never been to him to tell him we were seeking shelter in his house. My father did not believe the old villain, but he got him off.

One morning, while out driving, my parents came across the lady who was with the British force through the siege (Mrs. Tytler refused to leave her husband who was on duty with the troops). She told them she was on the way to the palace "treasure seeking," having gained the permission of the authorities to do so, and suggested that they should also apply for a digging ticket, or pass, which would enable them to go anywhere in the city to seek for treasure. My mother was delighted at the idea and quite excited over it, for it was well known that the city held much that was valuable which was hastily buried and hidden during the siege.

Here was the opportunity to regain our lost fortune! Directly they got home a letter was despatched for the magic piece of pasteboard that would work the oracle, and in due time it arrived.

Meanwhile my mother set to work to hunt up a really reliable, trustworthy native, who knew the city well, who would bring her news of where treasure was likely to be found, as she had no knowledge of the city and would have lost herself in the maze of streets and by-lanes. After some delay a suitable man presented himself and brought with him his own *coolies* armed with shovels and pickaxes, and the search commenced.

Every morning, after an early breakfast, accompanied by the guide, his men, and a government *peon* carrying a couple of iron rods (for sounding purposes) my parents started off to some place where fabulous wealth was said to be concealed. Every evening (about 3 or 4 p.

m.) saw them return looking fagged and tired, saddened and embittered by the sights they had seen and the tales they had been told, bringing only a few handsome shawls and eastern stuffs, vessels of silver and copper, a few precious stones and curious carvings—nothing very valuable.

My mother was beginning to feel disheartened and told the guide she thought him a fraud, and if he did not speedily lead her to the houses where the real treasure was concealed she would dismiss him; but he begged her to let him stay (for he had been promised a good reward if anything worth having was discovered) and pointed out to her that there was much room for search yet, and in the end she would be repaid if she persevered; so the digging continued. One day they went to a wretched little place in the heart of the city, where the streets were narrow and dark, and choked with rubbish and refuse—a foul, evil smelling, fearsome looking spot where any cruel deed might be committed and no one be a bit the wiser. Here the guide paused beside a narrow doorway that led into a dismal enclosure.

My parents looked at each other aghast! Did he expect them to go in there! Apparently, he did for he led the way. The government *peon* and *coolies* followed, so they went in too.

The place was empty and in ruins. Inside the high enclosure of stone walls was a narrow passage which had several niches in the walls, about two feet long, and one foot wide and about one foot in depth. They walked through this to the dark poky rooms beyond, and after a fruitless search here were returning through the passage very much disappointed and disgusted. The treasure was here sure enough, the guide declared, and must be found. So, they set to work with the rods tapping the floor all over but no hollow sound greeted their ears. Next, they tried the walls. These seemed solid enough. Evidently the guide had misled them again.

They were turning to go when my mother noticed that some of the niches were filled up with onions. She pointed this out to my father as strange in a deserted house. He immediately made a lunge with his rod at the onions which fell to the floor, and at the same time there was the unmistakable chink of silver! Smothered in the onions and completely hidden from sight were seven long bags filled with gold and silver coins! Inside one of the bags was a slip of paper on which was inscribed in Urdu characters "Seven vats, five pigeons!" The guide puzzled over the writing and thought it referred to the amount of treasure on the spot. The "Seven vats" meant the niches in which the bags were found, but the "five pigeons" had yet to be discovered. The place was carefully searched, but nothing more was found there.

One day they came upon a beautiful Agate bath, which they said, had found its way from the palace into the city (it had belonged to the king) and on several occasions they brought home handsome Indian jewellery, beautiful silver (inlaid) boxes, *pan dans*, *hooka* stands, silver vessels, small bags filled with money and precious stones and ancient coins, etc.

On the last day of the search my mother met with a remarkable adventure, and was the means (all unwittingly) of bringing to justice a notorious rebel ringleader, who was said to have escaped from the palace, and been killed on the day of the storming of the city walls.

My father was not very well that morning and unable to go with the party, so my mother went off without him (arming the government *peon* with a *talwar*, and carrying a pistol and ammunition herself). They drove in a new direction and had soon to get out and walk, for here the houses were closely packed, and the streets so narrow that no conveyance could pass through them. They had to go through this labyrinth of streets in single file, till they came to a small open square where there was a well, and overhanging this an ancient tamarind tree. This piece of ground was entirely surrounded by lofty houses with little more than paths leading to them. Some of the houses seemed to be occupied.

Right opposite the gully from which they had emerged stood a gateway. They made for this, and passing through stopped at a narrow door which the guide said was the entrance to the house that had to be searched. As my mother moved towards it a tall imposing looking Mohomedan confronted her, and deliberately blocked the way, insolently demanding what she wanted there! In a trice she whipped out the pistol and had it ready, and asked him "who he was." To which he replied in an offhand tone *Khuda ka banda* (The slave of God) and continued: "This is my home, and I refuse to admit you."

As he said this her eye fell on a splendid gold and *Sulumani* (onyx) bead necklace the fellow was wearing which was partly concealed by his thick dark beard. My mother knew that these stones are only supposed to be worn by "King or beggar;" and the man was no *fakir*, whatever else he might be, for he wore the ordinary garb of a Mussulman of the middle class.

"How came you by that necklace? You have no right to wear it." she said boldly, for she saw fanaticism and deadly hate in his eyes.

He took no notice of her question regarding the necklace but calmly remarked. "You are very wise, yet *Insha Ala Tala* (by the grace of the Almighty) I will outwit you." As he made this retort, he slowly stroked his beard (in token of a secret oath taken) and she saw he was no commoner, and meant to give trouble.

Nothing daunted, she called the government *peon* to her side. "Now," she said, "hand that necklace over to this man, and stand aside at once or I shall shoot you."

He quietly undid the clasp, laid the necklace in the *peon's* hands, laughed in a mocking manner saying "You will find nothing more today" and disappeared.

They went into the miserable place which was quite empty, lit a lantern and searched every nook and corner and then descended to the *thykana* (vault) which was pitch dark. Here they sounded the floor all over and fixed upon a spot to dig. After they had made a hole some six feet deep, they came upon a large stone slab some six feet long. This was lifted with difficulty (for it was thick and heavy), and underneath lay a full-size human skeleton in all its ghastliness! My mother never forgot the evil odour which, pervaded the place as the stone was removed, and the awful sight that met her eyes. Faint and sick, she hurried out of the wretched place, leaving the *coolies* to fill up the grave. She was too ill and upset for any more digging that day, and deaf to the entreaties of the guide who wanted her to go back and have the bones removed; for he declared that "untold wealth lay there" and the skeleton could be replaced and covered up after it had been removed. On the way home he told her what he thought of the Mohamedan who had questioned their right to enter the house.

"That man," he said, "is a great man in disguise—he *knew* the treasure was there, and would probably be searched for, so *he* had the skeleton placed over it to frighten people away. If the *huzoor* will permit me to look beneath at once it will be found; otherwise that man who is guarding it will remove it during the night."

But she felt she could not face such an ordeal without my father, especially as the man looked a dangerous character, and had threatened her; so she told the guide that the *Sahib* would accompany them next morning, and it would be all right, at which he smiled and said it would be too late. When she reached home, she hastened to relate the adventure to my father, telling him that she was quite certain the Mussulman was no mean character, and should be looked after. My father wrote to the officials at once, with the result that the man was tracked and captured, found to be the very one they wanted, and sent to the gallows.

The necklace proved a beauty; the stones, some of them, of extraordinary size and magnificence. These were set in gold and made into brooches, the smaller ones into rings and given away as "Mutiny souvenirs" to those who had shown us kindness in our time of need. The agate bath was also turned into such useful articles as pen trays, trinket boxes, etc. Most of these were also given to friends. What was in that dreadful place was left to its grim guardian, for my parents did not care to renew the search. They were quite content, and well able to start afresh, though a portion of what fell to our lot was claimed by government. Some of the coins were very valuable, and brought us a small fortune. It was rather amusing to hear the experiences of some of the other "treasure seekers" for all were not as fortunate as my parents.

One old gentleman who was the proud possessor of very handsome silver plate, which he had to leave behind when he fled the day of the outbreak, never tired of bemoaning his loss, and wearying others with his sad complainings, when he returned after the siege. In his excitement and delight over the search for treasure the plate went quite out of his mind, till one day while digging in some spot where he had been told some jewellery of great value was buried, he came upon one of his own spoons! He recovered nearly all the plate, but the treasure (to him) was a myth,

We were lucky in getting a good, honest guide, who faithfully did his duty (and was amply rewarded for it) though, as he often told us, he had made many enemies in the city over the business, for he went as a spy amongst his own kindred, and learnt all he could from them, and then led my parents to places he was certain of; and had my mother set scruples aside, and gone back that day and looked *under* the skeleton, she would, no doubt, have found a fortune there.

Mrs. Tytler, too, was very lucky. She had the palace as her hunting ground, and to her lot fell some beautiful ornaments belonging to the king's family, as also the wonderful silken garment the king wore all through the siege, which had the *Koran* printed minutely all over. This was said to be a talisman against evil. The old fellow lost faith in its power the day the British entered the city, and cast it aside.

We were more than repaid for all our losses on the terrible day, the 11th of May. Our house was re-built on the same foundation, and filled with all the wonderful things my parents collected in those eventful days—rich from floor to ceiling with the spoils. Eastern stuffs which made handsome *pardas*, curious metal-ware and many other things too numerous to detail, which were found lying about pell-mell in the murky houses and dirty streets and gullies, mostly costly and valuable. But my dear simple-minded father took far more delight in digging up relics of the siege—he had quite a collection of weapons of every description, and spent and flattened bullets, and shot. Each told its own tale of that wonderful storming of a great city with impregnable walls, swarming with a well-armed host of fanatical foes which were overcome, worsted and driven out by a handful of determined self-reliant Europeans, and to him Nicholson was no less a *Guru* (saint) and hero than he was to the Sikh, *for he* was the soul of that army.

Among our relics—my father's chief treasures, (which he took a delight in showing to the many who came about us curious to hear the narrative of our wonderful escape) were first the old family Bible, (which had been tossed about and flung in the Kudsia Gardens, and which I have still), next a miniature lizard, cut out of a *single splendid emerald*—flawless, in its beauty, and an earthen cup, in which some milk was brought for me at Panipat, (which I refused to touch, because it *was* an earthen cup). This cup was kept to drink from on that dreadful journey to Karnal and is now in my possession. And—(I was forgetting) the deadly knives, bullets and weapons of war. My mother used to laugh at these for her tastes were different and she had many beautiful things to show, and I think those who came to see us preferred to look over and admire her portion of the spoils.

There were others who escaped from Delhi, whom we met years after the mutiny, who told us the tales of their miraculous escapes. These are therefore quite authentic.

MRS. LEESON'S NARRATIVE.

The lady mentioned by Wilberforce in his book (a missing chapter of the Indian Mutiny) was a member of the Collins and Staines' family who nearly all perished during that terrible time, most of them on the morning of the outbreak.

On the morning of the 11th May, the members of this family, in common with all the Europeans in Delhi, were alarmed by the report that mutineers from Meerut had entered the city and were massacring the Europeans. They consequently all assembled in a fine house which belonged to one of them near the Church, and close to the city wall. The house had a *tykhana* or deep underground apartment made for coolness in the hot weather, the floor of which, though much below the level of the ground within the city, was on a level with that on the outside of the walls, and with which it communicated by a small door pierced through the city wall. Thither they descended to the number of about thirty, including children and infants. There they remained during the whole of the 11th May, while the massacre was going on above (the noise of which they heard, including the explosion of the magazine), but on the morning of the 12th the cries of the children for food forced them from their concealment.

Their house was close to the Water Bastion, one face of which looked towards the ridge where the British Army afterwards en-camped, while the other, in which was the door before mentioned, looked towards the river. Through this door they all passed, and went along between the wall and the river till they came to a small arched gateway, but without a gate on it, in the city wall, and leading into the city. At this archway they found two *sepoys*, who said that they had orders to bring them all to the palace before the king. They accord-ingly brought them inside the city wall again, and led them up to what are now the Government College grounds, which were then covered with dense bushes. As they were going up here in loose order, one of the *sepoys* shot one of the women, and her two little daughters crying out "Oh, they have shot mamma!" ran away to hide themselves among the bushes, but the *sepoy* followed and shot them too.

Mrs. Leeson's account of what followed was most pathetic, but considering that there were several men among the party, most unac-countable. She said that the *sepoys* loaded their muskets and shot them deliberately down, one after another, as they walked quietly along, none of them apparently except the first two little girls, making any attempt to escape, either by running away or by attacking the two *sepoys*. They seemed overwhelmed by the idea of *kismet* or fate and as she was walking quietly up to the tank in the college grounds to get a drink, and carrying her baby, one of the *sepoys* shot her.

The bullet went through the baby and through her too; and she fell close to the tank, and of course could tell no more.

Her two other children were doubtless murdered there too. There she lay for one hour or two, till a young Afghan who was learning to be a *moulvie*, or priest, and was living for this purpose with an old *moulvie* in the city, came and found her. He said "it is right to kill the men but not right to kill the women and children." So, he gave her a drink, and brought a sheet and spread it over her.

He watched by her during the burning heat of the day, supplying her occasionally with water, and at night brought a light native bedstead and had her conveyed to his master's house. There she recovered, the only survivor of the large company who had passed the night in the *tykhana*, and there she remained during almost the whole siege.

At the *moulvie's* house she found herself in very different surroundings. She was now in a native *havalie* lying on a *charpai,* her wounds roughly bound and bandaged and dark faces about her. The sight of these made her shrink with terror, but she was soon assured that she was quite safe with them, and would be treated as one of themselves. Their ways and habits and mode of life are so different to ours, and it was sometime before she could reconcile herself to the many peculiarities of the household, and above all, to get over her fear and aversion to the dark faces who tended her and ministered to her wants. In them she saw the murderers of her children, the ruthless, heartless creatures who had deprived her, in one short hour, of home and kin—and she found it hard to realise that they meant kindly by her. Moreover, there were rumours of trouble all round, and the uncertainty of her husband's fate made her brood over the past and the desire to live grew less day by day. Fever set in, and there was a time when she was back again in her home surrounded by all that made life dear to her—The voices of her loved ones in her ears.

All the time she lay listless and impassive, slowly recovering from her wound, and the fever which subsequently followed from exposure and weakness. The army of retribution was forming itself and advancing upon Delhi. This, too, was whispered to her by the women who pitied her for her youth and helplessness, and all she had suffered. She was told that there would be a great fight soon, and it was possible that they would have to move to a more sheltered part of the city; in that case what would they do with her? It was boasted that the English would never be able to retake the city and set foot inside the gates!

All these babblings fell on listless ears. She felt she was an alien, and, in their power, that at any moment in spite of their tolerance of her, that the hatred to her race was too deeply grafted to be completely veiled, and she could see they were only waiting the course of events. Should the English be victorious they might restore her to her own people. If they failed it would mean death, or worse, and so in the midst of sorrow and suffering and uncertainty, with little to hope for, and less to live for, the days sped on apace. They almost persuaded her to accept their faith, and repeat the *kulma* (creed) urging that should there be no rescue she would have to remain with them and become a Mussalman, but for all her weakness and misery she said she would rather die in her own faith.

One morning the *moulvie* appeared very much disturbed and unsettled. The women too kept together, whispering in an excited manner and from vague hints they let fall she gathered that the English troops were victorious, and were marching on the ridge. She felt in those days that her fate was in the balance, but the good tidings had brought her strength, and the desire to *live*, and return to her own people; so she entreated them to restore her to the English and promised to have them rewarded for all the kindness they had shown her. They said they were only waiting for the opportunity. One morning she was told to dress herself in a suit, of clothes that was given her, and to join the *moulvie* outside the walls of the *zenana*. Thus disguised (as an Afghan) she was put into a *bylee* (oxcart) and driven off.

The siege had now lasted for some months, and the British troops occupied the ridge and the *subzee-mundi*. They were so few in number, however, that only a small portion of the city walls near the Kashmere and Lahore gates was attacked by them; all the rest of the city walls was unmolested, and ingress and egress to and from the city was as free as in times of peace. It was indeed a marvellous siege and speaks volumes for British pluck, dash, and endurance. The *bylee* with Mrs. Leeson in it passed slowly through the narrow streets. The few who made enquiries about it were told that a native lady was going to another place. They passed out through the Delhi gate and took the road to the British camp near the *subzee-mundi*, a few bullets pattering around them but doing no harm. As they were nearing the camp, they saw a number of grass-cutters going for water, hailed them and let them know who they were.

As soon as the grass-cutters knew they had come from the city, they rushed away and gave the alarm in camp. An officer (Major Chalmers) came and received her, and brought her to General Nicholson. She told her story to Nicholson who, however, would not believe it. He would not believe that a Christian woman could live so many months in Delhi; and told her, much to her indignation, that she was a spy! but he nevertheless put her in charge of the only European lady in camp (Mrs. Tytler). There she remained for a few days and was then sent off to Meerut, where she was ultimately joined by her husband who was at Agra during the outbreak.

Mrs. Leeson was not the only Christian woman who was in the city during the siege. There was another who was saved by *sepoys*.

When the Meerut troopers entered the city and the massacre began, she, her child, and a number of Europeans, men, and women, were taken prisoners and led to the fort. The area of the fort was then filled with native houses built generally round little courts, and into one of these they were all put for the night. This court was also occupied by some of the mutinous *sepoys*, who, attracted by the little girl's prattle, showed her some kindness, and when orders came for the prisoners to be brought before the king, they concealed her and her child under a *charpai* and covered them with a sheet. The others, surrounded by *sepoys*, holding a rope to prevent escape, were taken before the king and his two sons, who were seated in the magnificent Dewan Khas, or hall of private audience.

The old king was in his dotage and a mere puppet; but the two villainous sons, who were afterwards so deservedly shot by Hodgson, ordered them all to be put to death, and they were accordingly murdered then and there before their eyes. The poor woman remained in the court with the *sepoys* who told her they couldn't conceal her for long, but treated her kindly. One evening they told her she would be murdered next day as their regiment was ordered out to fight. They went, and like all the rest, came back beaten; but during their absence no one molested her. She remained with them all through the siege, and when the city was stormed, and the mutineers quitted it, they left her unharmed.

In contrast to those who quietly submitted to their fate on that terrible day, and made no resistance were a few who pluckily held their own, and died fighting to the last. Of these the Berresford family (mother and daughters) kept their assailants at bay with spears, wounding several of the rebels before they were overpowered by them, and fell mortally wounded themselves. The bungalow, which is now No. 5 Duryagung, was held for three days by a few plucky men, and they would have held out longer had ammunition not failed them. Duryagung was the first part of Delhi that the mutineers from Meerut attacked and as this house was the only one capable of defence, the Christians from the neighbouring houses sought refuge in it. It was occupied by Mr. Aldwell and his family.

Those who took shelter in it were—

Revd. Mackay (Baptist Missionary), Conductor Nolan, Sub-Conductor Settle, Sergeant Connors, Mrs. Nolan and three children; Mrs. Riley and two children; Mrs. Crowe and three children; Mrs. Davis and two daughters. Mrs. Prince, Mrs. Foulan, Mr. A. G. Aldwell, A,

Aldwell, and J. S. Aldwell.

The house had two storeys. The women and children were placed in the lower rooms with Revd. Mackay. The doors were then bolted and barricaded, and every available piece of furniture piled against them. The men six in number then went upstairs, carrying their guns and ammunition with them, Sub-Conductor Nolan took command of the small band, and prepared for defence.

The servants had all left after breaking all the *surais* and water *chattis* in the house! About 10 o'clock a Muhammadan *dyer* entered the compound flourishing a bloody *talwar*, and calling on the *kaffirs* to come out and be killed! He was told to go away but persisted in his wild evolutions before the gate, so he was shot down. All that day, strange to say, no one else molested them, though all round there was rioting and turmoil. After sunset the hospital guard fell in and the native doctor left the place. The *sepoys* sent the sick away and after taking whatever they wanted, they fired a parting volley at No. 5 bungalow and marched off. The city rabble now rushed into the hospital, and started breaking the medicine bottles and looting it, and wound up by setting the place on fire. About midnight there was a great noise and the rumble of wheels, so they knew they were going to have their turn next.

It was bright moonlight which showed the front of the house to the mutineers. The gate leading into the compound was a bamboo one. This had been fastened, and large stones placed against it to prevent its being pushed open.

The mutineers brought four guns and placed them in position about 30 yards from the gate.

The order was given to load, and as each gun was loaded it was fired. They fired about a dozen shots, all flew overhead, wide of the mark—not one struck the house. They then depressed the guns, and the shot struck the top of the house, while the infantry fired volleys at it. Conductor Nolan now gave the order to "let them have it" which was heartily responded to and the six rifles on the roof rang out, and as many rebels bit the dust. At this they left their guns and ran to shelter, when the fire from the house ceased, they came back to reload and fire (this time with grape and cannister) about 4 a.m. they retired, kept away all day and returned at midnight to renew the attack, bringing a large body of infantry with them. About 3 a.m. Conductor Settle was killed.

All this time this gallant band of Europeans had been without food and water and now the ammunition was giving out, powder and shot they had in plenty, but the bullets were nearly expended and the succour from Meerut that they had so relied on had failed them! On the morning of the 13th at 4 a.m. it was decided to abandon the place, and if possible, escape to the river bank (where there was dense jungle) and hide. Conductor Nolan placed Mr. Aldwell and his son James to defend the entrance leading to the ramparts, and Sergeant Connors and Mr. A. Aldwell to keep up a steady fire at the enemy from behind the wall over the steps down which the women and children were to pass, but the rebels seemed to guess their intention for they now directed their guns at the steps, and the second salvo destroyed these, entirely cutting off their chance of escape.

The *sepoys*, in numbers now rushed the house and made a dash for the veranda to get under cover from the two guns above. Seeing it was all over and they had broken into the house Mr. Aldwell and his son jumped down and managed to reach the ramparts, ran along these to the Wellesly bastion, from thence to the berm from the embrasure facing the Delhi gate and escaped, the only two who left the place alive. The rest were brutally murdered, and their bodies thrown into the ditch beneath the walls.

One young officer we knew was attacked by rebels, and defended himself as long as he was able to do so, till his sword was knocked out of his hand. Then they cut him down and left him for dead (with those he had killed in the encounter) on the bridge where he fell, under which there was some water. When he came to his senses all was still and quiet, find it was bright moonlight. At first, he could not recollect what had occurred, or how he came to be there, then the pain of his wounds (he had several) brought it all back to him and he realised that he had been left for dead. Thus, he lay for some time till a great thirst overpowered him and he started to crawl towards the water under the bridge.

Twice overcome by pain he swooned—recovered—to drag himself nearer and nearer, and at length reached the brink of the muddy, unwholesome pool in which some buffaloes were wallowing. The drink revived him, and he lay in the cool damp earth near the water and wondered when death would come and relieve him of his terrible sufferings. Jackals prowled about and raised their weird cry, waxing bolder as their numbers increased, but his strength was spent, and he found he could not move hand or foot to scare them. He tried to shout, and succeeded in uttering some sort of a sound that sent them scurrying away to attack the carcases on the bridge.

At length he heard footsteps, but these might be the enemy come to look after their dead and rather than fall into their hands alive, he summoned the little strength left him, and with an effort rolled over on his side right among the buffaloes into the water which was shallow near the brink. The footsteps stopped on the bridge above and he heard a voice which he knew well say, "Ah, My *Sahib!* I tell you it was here I saw them surround him, *here he fell,* and living or dead we must find him!" It was his orderly who had seen him cut down on the bridge and (with another trooper) had come to look for him.

"Meer Khan," he feebly cried, "I am here under the bridge."

The man heard his own name uttered in an unearthly tone, and seeming to proceed from the depths beneath, and a superstitious fear almost got the better of him. His companion heard it too and said, in an awed whisper: "It was his spirit that spoke let us begone!" but the orderly rallied and answered.

"If his spirit spoke, then his body surely must be near, and we must find it, and give it a resting place lest the spirit trouble us in years to come!"

Then they heard their master's voice this time quite clear and distinct calling them to his aid under the bridge. Guided by the sound, they at length found him, carried him to the camp, and he recovered from his wounds.

About five years after the mutiny an attempt was made on my poor father's life—who by, was never ascertained, for there was no clue to the dastardly perpetrator of the cruel deed.

We were spending the summer at Simla in a house called "North View" below the mall. As it was a large double-storeyed place we only occupied the lower half. The upstairs rooms were engaged by a firm of merchants who had a showroom above. I was then old enough to go to a day school and was not at home when the terrible thing occurred, but I shall never forget that awful day, and the time of sorrow and anxiety that followed, and the fearful consternation the event created—not only in our own home, but in all Simla where our family was well known and we had many relatives and friends.

It happened after breakfast. My father, mother and eldest stepsister were in the front veranda. My father stood a little apart smoking a cigar near the veranda railings, looking down the *khud* beneath, which was densely wooded with tall firs and oaks. On the left of the house there was a hill on which there were a few houses dotted about (for

Simla was not so crowded then). This hill too was a forest of pines. My mother and sister were seated looking at a *boxwalla's* wares which he had spread out on the floor at their feet. Suddenly my father threw up his arms and exclaimed "Oh God, I am shot!" and tottered, and simultaneously there was the loud report of a gun. My sister rushed to my father's side to support him, while my mother in a frenzy ran out of the veranda to see who had fired, calling for help as she ran. My sister supported and helped my poor father to his room, tore off his coat and vest, as she did so, a spout of blood squirted on to her face and dress.

The first doctor who arrived happened to be a visitor to Simla (Doctor Fowler, 82nd Regiment), he told my sister what to do, but would not examine the wound till the Civil Surgeon came. When Doctor Clarke (the Civil Surgeon) arrived, he attended to the wound and found that the bullet had entered the chest within an inch of the heart, and passed right out beneath the shoulder blade at the back, so that there were two wounds to dress! When I returned from school about 3 p.m., I shall never forget the sight that met my eyes! The road from the mall to the house was crowded by people going to and fro; amongst these was General Crawford Chamberlain who stopped me and asked me to ride home with him to lunch. He did not allude to the fearful thing that had occurred (and as I was often invited to the Chamberlains, with whom I was a great pet, I saw nothing unusual in the invitation or the general's manner) so making some excuse I rode on to the house.

There in the compound and veranda were a crowd of Europeans and natives of all classes, who made way for me, but none of these said a word about the accident though they looked pityingly and kindly, and some addressed me as I passed on into the house. The hall, or passage was also choked with people—all seemed very much excited and stood about in groups whispering. The stillness, with all those people about seemed to awe me, young as I was, and I felt something was wrong! Presently my sister came out of my father's room covered with blood, and I could see that she had been crying, and then I was told of the awful thing that had happened.

She took me away to the nursery, where my little brother (in charge of his nurse) was playing quietly with his toys, impressed upon me the necessity for keeping very quiet "or papa would never get well." I stayed there for a short time asking the nurse what had happened to my dear father, but she would not enlighten me, so I crept out through the back veranda to the other side of the house where my father's room lay. The room had a low, wide window, which was always kept open at the head of his bed; from this window standing on tiptoe I could just see into the room. There lay my father stripped to the waist with an ugly wound two doctors were bending over and attending to. Here I would have stayed frozen in misery and horror, had I not been observed and carried back to the nursery, and shut in there for the rest of the day.

It was months before my poor father recovered from this accident (if such it could be called). There were several doctors in Simla. All saw the wounds, and held a consultation over the case and all differed as to the nature of the wounds, the majority were of the opinion that the bullet had entered in front and come out at the back, but Doctor Farquar (Sir John Lawrence's physician, who was sent by Lord Lawrence to report daily on the case) held out that the shot had been fired from *behind* at a distance of about 50 yards or so, and whoever had done it must have aimed deliberately to take life.

The police laid hands on a small boy who was after birds or monkeys with a rook rifle, but he was set free at once, for his small gun could never have caused such a wound. My mother's views on the subject pointed to Indian intrigue, and I think she was right for natives are very revengeful and vindictive. I must not forget to mention a pleasing incident that occurred about this time. Sir Colin Campbell was then chief of the army in India.

He had been told our wonderful tale, and was much impressed by it. At a crowded assemblage he took the opportunity of publicly expressing his appreciation of my parents' heroism and gallant fight for life against desperate odds.

He and his staff rode up to my mother, and the chief presented a magnificent bouquet to her, remarking as he did so, that "he wished he could have the pleasure of presenting her with the cross for valour, for if ever a woman deserved it, she did!"

He afterwards showed us much kindness, and when he was leaving India for good some years later, he made a present of his favourite *Yarkandi* pony, and an easy chair (which he said had been a great comfort to him during his term of service out here) to my father—for he said he did not wish anyone else to have these. The pony was called "Clyde" after his late master and became a great pet in the household.

My Recollections of the Sepoy Revolt

Colonel and Mrs. Dunbar Douglas Muter

Contents

To
My Beloved Husband
Dunbar Douglas Muter
Colonel
Who entered into rest October 7th, l909
These Pages are Dedicated
by His Devoted Wife and Companion
for 55 Years
Through an Eventful and
Very Unusual Career

Preface

The approaching pageant—the proposed Coronation Durbar at Delhi—which promises to be an historical event in the annals of Great Britain and of India, affords a fitting occasion on which to recall and to contrast the picture presented on that site in 1857 and in 1911.

Then, the struggle for Empire fell to the lot of a few brave and resolute spirits nerved by duty to "fight to the finish," or to die, in face of overwhelming difficulties of climate, and of opposing numbers in a strongly fortified walled city.

Now, our king and queen will hold High Court on the battlefield rendered sacred by the sacrifices made by the "Delhi Field Force," surrounded by a brilliant retinue of native and loyal princes of high rank.

11, Park Street,
Windsor

Part 1: Outbreak at Meerut—To Fall of Delhi

CHAPTER 1

On Sunday, May 10th, 1857, I was at Meerut. The 1st Battalion 60th King's Royal Rifles, in which my husband was then a captain, occupied the Infantry barracks. The men were parading for church at about 6.30 p.m. My husband had left me to accompany them. The sun was sinking in a blaze of fiery heat that rose hazy and glowing from the baked plain. I drove to the church and waited outside the door, expecting every moment to hear the sound of a gay march which so strangely heralds the approach of a body of soldiers to divine worship; but— I listened in vain. A dull sound, very different from that I expected, came over the stillness of Nature around; but I little heeded the holiday-making in the *bazaars*, holiday-making, as I then thought it, though it was the commencement of a saturnalia destined to take a place in history and to revolutionise the great Empire we had founded in the East.

A gentleman accosted me. "You need not be alarmed, but an outbreak has taken place requiring the presence of the troops, so there will not be a service in the church this evening."

"A slight disturbance would not stop the service," I replied; "therefore I will wait a little."

But when the clock struck seven, the hour to commence, and no congregation was assembling, I called to my friend and requested him to tell my husband, should he arrive, that he had advised me to return home. Up to this, I was seated with my back to the cantonment in a little pony carriage, but the moment the horses' heads were turned I saw the native lines in a blaze, and, in some alarm, but not in the least understanding the gravity of the position, I gave the order to hasten home.

The sun had set and was quickly followed by the dusk which leaves so little space in this region between the glare of day and the darkness of night. I faced in the direction of the native lines, and now in terror and amazement beheld the horizon on fire as if the whole cantonment were in flames. Entering the broad road that leads to the *bazaar* I saw it was crowded with men.

Two of the European artillery were hurrying up, pursued by a throng of natives hurling every missile they could get at the wounded and unarmed Englishmen. So intent were they on this occupation that I was allowed to pass uninjured into a road leading to my house. Our servants were assembled at the gate in a flutter of alarm, the *khansamah* (answering to a house steward) at their head. He declared he could no longer be responsible for any property, and bringing the silver in use, he returned it to my charge. At the same time, he advised me to conceal myself—a proposal he saw I regarded as an insult. To conceal myself in my own house, in the lines of a regiment that had reckoned up a century of renown! And from what? That was the question. Was the Native Army in revolt? Had the threatened storm come so soon, and was the instrument so carefully sharpened by our government at its own throat?

The distant roar now rolled up a babel of voices, nearly drowning the ceaseless rattle of musketry, and above all came the heavy tramp of an English battalion on the march, which can be distinguished at once from the movement of any other body by one accustomed to the sound.

The interview with my servants was interrupted by a sergeant sent by my husband with directions for me to proceed to the quarter guard. He told me the native force had broken into revolt, that they were shooting down every European they met, and that the English troops were moving on the *bazaars*. With drawn swords (already armed) the *chokedhar* (our night-watchman) and the *khansamah* escorted me, one on either side, to the place indicated, where I found many fugitives already assembled. Beyond the outer approach my escort declined to proceed, saying the soldiers would kill them.

"Not," I replied, "if you are doing no harm. But, *khansamah*, I hold you personally responsible for everything in my house."

He made me a grand *salaam*, and on his return to our bungalow, though in ordinary times scrupulously honest, he forced open some cases recently soldered, preparatory to our intended departure for the hills, believing that neither Colonel Muter nor I would ever return alive to the house, and proceeded to make a selection from the contents.

The scene at the quarter guard was not calculated to strengthen my fortitude. Fearful rumours were rapidly circulated, and as rapidly followed by others still more dreadful, a favourite being that the silver ornaments on the belt of the officers of the 60th formed an excellent mark, and that as soon as the officers had been killed the battalion would become disorganised and helpless. With such talk around me, I was glad to escape to a room close by, kindly offered to me by the wife of a pay-sergeant.

Every moment added to the noise, and through the roar of countless voices came the boom of heavy guns: one, two, three— then silence, and these dread messengers of good and evil tidings ceased for that night.

In the midst of the confusion a stranger presented himself with his family, directed by my husband to join me. His house situated in the *bazaar* had, with all its contents, been burnt to the ground, and the family had narrowly escaped. The servants had concealed them under boughs of trees in the garden, whence they witnessed the destruction of their property, and heard the savage demand made by the armed ruffians for the discovery of their retreat. When hope had almost vanished, the place had been cleared by a party of the Rifles, and they had been sent under escort to our house, whence they were directed to the quarter guard. Before midnight the troops reached the Mall, where they bivouacked, throwing a chain of sentries around the European lines; and as I could then do so in safety, I returned to my house, accompanied by the fugitives.

All that night I walked on the veranda, watching the flames as they sprang up from the burning houses. I could see in the new fires the progress of the incendiaries, who sometimes approached, as I thought, perilously near our lines. The weary night ended, the last flames died out ere the rising sun reddened the sky; and I retired to rest, with the impression of an event stamped on my mind no time can erase.

The sun rose on a scene changed in a manner words cannot describe. It was not only that it had sunk on a peaceful parade for church and rose on blackened ruins and murdered Christians; it had also sunk on good and kindly feelings, and now rose on the wildest storm of man's passions. It was mid-day turned to black night—a picture of peace changed by magic to one of war. We felt intuitively that it was a great revolution—a cyclone that had merely its centre at Meerut, destined to sweep with a violence that would startle the world, over the length and breadth of the land. Perhaps the framework of English rule would go down before the tempest, and, if so, what fate was reserved for us?

The Rifles on that Sunday evening had assembled on the parade ground. The men were standing in groups, ready to "fall in" on the sound of the bugle, and the officers were scattered in little knots, when suddenly a stream of soldiers poured tumultuously towards their barrack-rooms.

"What is the matter?" was the general exclamation.

"The *sepoys* are in mutiny," was the answer.

Without orders, the parade was changed. The men had been waiting, without arms, for divine service—they now came forth armed and accoutred for action. Colonel Muter, then a junior captain in the battalion, in the absence of senior officers, instantly despatched the company of Riflemen first ready and equipped, to the *bazaar*, to secure the Treasury and the records—who, coming up "at the double," arrived just as the native guard, twice their strength, had turned out irresolute. This Lieutenant Austin, my husband's subaltern, settled for them, ordering them to "ground arms," and all that night the *kutchery* was surrounded by a howling mob who found the Treasury, containing some *lakhs* of *rupees*, beyond their reach, while incendiarism was checked in that quarter.

By this timely action not only the Meerut Cantonment, but the whole Meerut district, enjoyed regular pay during this distracted period, and many ladies called on me on our return to Meerut, after the winter spent in Delhi, to express their thanks to my husband for the comfort his prompt action had secured for them. The value of the treasure thus saved may in some measure be imagined when the size of the district is considered; also, the strength of the garrison at Meerut, which consisted of 1st Battalion 60th King's Royal Rifles, 6th Dragoon Guards and Bengal Artillery—all Europeans, and three native regiments, two infantry and one cavalry. In many works on this Mutiny surprise is expressed that in Meerut alone the usual course was departed from, and the Treasury escaped the invariable spoliation, unaware that its rescue from attack was due to my husband.

★★★★★★

In the preface to his *History of the Indian Mutiny*, Fifth Edition, published Dec. 6th, 1903, Mr. T. Rice Holmes, courteously gives credit to Colonel Muter for having, by his prompt action, saved the Treasury at Meerut at the time of the outbreak.

******

In Kaye's excellent *History of the Sepoy War* (Vol. 2) the remark occurs:—

> Always the same experience, the mutineers made for the gaol, released the prisoners, plundered the Treasury, destroyed the *kutchery* with all its records, and gutted houses of the Christian inhabitants.

At Allahabad £170,000 in silver was taken. At Cawnpore on the night of 4th June the 2nd native cavalry proceeded to the commissariat cattle-yards, took thirty-six elephants, the property of the Government, and went direct to the Treasury, some seven miles distant; and there, assisted by the Mahratta troops of the *Nana Sahib*, they plundered and carried off about eight and a half *lakhs* of *rupees*, which they packed on the elephants and in carts. All this was unknown as the programme of the mutineers at the time Colonel Muter took the first step in one of England's most memorable struggles.

Meanwhile, the convalescent, the excused, those going on pass—all rushed into the ranks; and the colonel who attended to march the men to church found the soldiers in column of route ready to engage an enemy. Thus, the first move made in one of England's most momentous wars was by the private soldiers, who seemed to have a keen appreciation of the crisis and of the work before them.

All the guards, save those over the quarters of the European forces, were given by the native infantry. Even in the lines of European regiments, Native sentries mounted over the quartermaster's stores. When the ammunition was sent for, the native guard was seen sneaking away. So rapidly had the 60th got under arms that they could with ease have captured all the natives on duty in their lines, but neither the officers nor the men had a notion of the length to which the Mutiny had proceeded, and they waited impatiently for orders to act.

In the meantime the surprise was so complete that the chief commissioner, Mr. Greathed, became aware of his danger only when men were yelling in tens of thousands around his house, and he was roused from his security to trust his own life and that of his wife into the hands of his servants, who safely carried them through that night of danger. The general escaped by a back way, and the brigadier rode at full speed from his home with the bullets of his own guard whistling past his head. Probably this officer—Sir Archdale Wilson—whose good fortune it was to strike the final blow at Delhi, never more

77

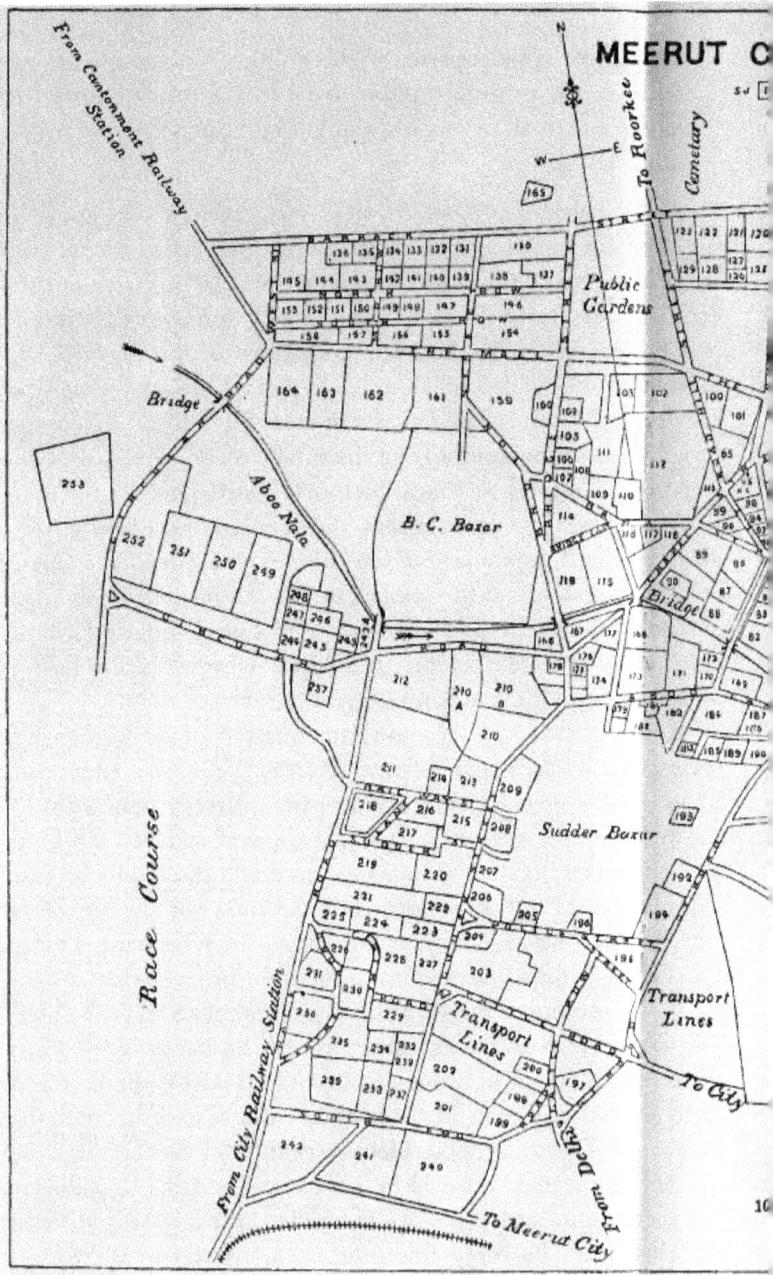

MEERUT C[ANTONMENT]

From Cantonment Railway Station

To Roorkee

Cemetary

N
W — E
S

165

Public Gardens

136 135 134 133 132 131 130
165 164 163 162 161 160 139 138 137
153 152 151 150 149 148 147 146
158 157 156 155 154

123 122 121 120
129 128 127 126

Bridge

164 163 162 141 159

166 108 107 102 100
105 111 101
106 100 107 65
105 110 112
114 99 96
116 112 118 97
119 115 89 88
90 20 87
Bridge 86

253

Aboo Nala

252 251 250 249

248
247 246
245
244 245 244

B. C. Bazar

168 167 171 168
179 176 173 172 171 170 149
134 172
184 187
185 188 189 190
193

237

212 210 A 210 B
210

211 214 213 209
218 216 215 208
217

Race Course

219 220 207
221 222 206
225 224 223 205 196
226 228 227 203
231 230 204
236 229 Transport Lines 200
235 234 232 239 202 197
235 233 237 201
242 241 240

Sudder Bazar

192
194
191

Transport Lines

To City

From City Railway Station

From Delhi

To Meerut City

10

Ⓧ 60ᵀᴴ RIFLE GUARD ROOM

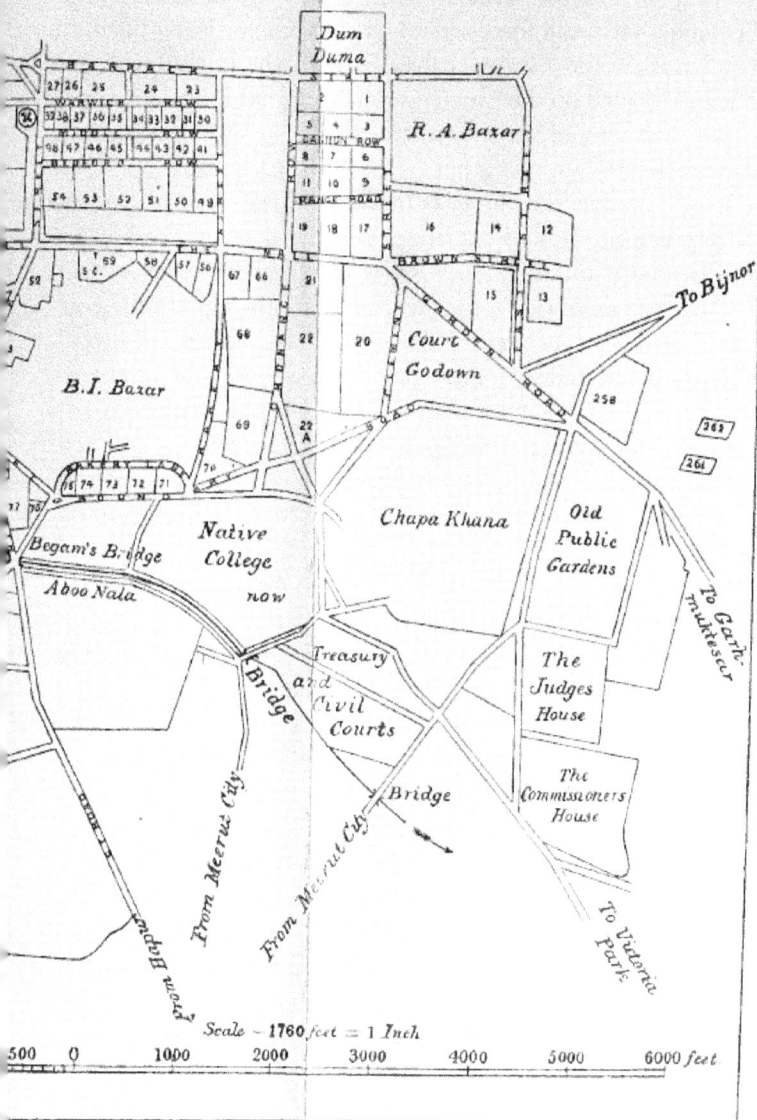

Dum
Duma

R. A. Bazar

HARRACK

| 27 | 26 | 25 | | 24 | | 23 |

WARWICK RLW.

| 39 | 38 | 37 | 36 | 35 | | 34 | 33 | 32 | 31 | 30 |

BEDFORD RLW.

| 48 | 47 | 46 | 45 | | 44 | 43 | 42 | 41 |

| 54 | 53 | 52 | 51 | 50 | 49 |

| 2 | | 1 |
| 5 | 4 | 3 |
BROWN ROW
| 8 | 7 | 6 |
| 11 | 10 | 9 |
RANGE ROAD
| 19 | 18 | 17 |

| 16 | | 14 | | 12 |

To Bijnor

| 59 | 58 | 57 | 56 |
| 52 |
| 69 | 68 | 67 | 66 | 21 |

BROWN ST.

| 15 | | 13 |

258

| 263 |
| 261 |

68 22 20 Court
Godown

B. I. Bazar

GARDEN ROAD

69 22
A

75 74 73 72 71
70

BAKERY
TOWN

Chapa Khana

Old
Public
Gardens

To Gari
muktesur

Begam's Bridge

Native
College
now

Aboo Nala

Treasury
and
Civil
Courts

The
Judges
House

Bridge

The
Commissioners
House

Bridge

From Meerut City

From Meerut City

From Hapur

To Victoria
Park

Scale - 1760 feet = 1 Inch

| 500 | 0 | | 1000 | 2000 | 3000 | 4000 | 5000 | 6000 feet |

nearly met his fate. While the chiefs were concealing themselves or riding for their lives, the *bazaars* were in the hands of myriads of *Goojurs* (plundering gipsy tribe) and *badmashes* (rogues and vagabonds in the city) who had assembled from the surrounding country to assist in the extermination of the English and to sack the cantonment. The brigadier rode up and the battalion moved at once on the *bazaar*. It was joined by a battery of artillery and some troops of cavalry. Fearing to entangle this small force among the dense masses that filled the streets and a native force stronger than his own, the general passed to the right and formed on the parade ground in front of the native lines.

The sun had set and the moon had not yet lit up the scene. The illumination before him rising out of the thick blackness around was one of awful grandeur. For more than a mile three rows of thatched bungalows were on fire, and the spaces between seemed filled with a legion of fiends. As the skirmishers drew close, mounted *sowars* with drawn sabres were seen riding furiously about in the light of the conflagration; but the troops approached in darkness, and it was not till the Enfield bullet in its deadly flight passed close by, that the mutineers knew their danger. Drawing rapidly to their left, the loud hum told the brigadier they were congregating on his right. Some guns were unlimbered and the multitude was dispersed with three rounds of grape. This was the last ever seen of the Native Army of Bengal in the lines of Meerut.

I propose to give a slight sketch of the cantonment, that what I have to record may be the better understood.

Meerut stands in the centre of the Doab, or territory between the Rivers Ganges and Jumna. The country from the ranges of the Himalaya for hundreds of miles towards Central India is an unvaried plain. Meerut is one of the oldest stations in India, and in years gone by was held by a division of troops so large as almost to be termed an army. Then it was a frontier post, but as the country advanced, so advanced the troops, leaving behind vast ranges of barracks, rows of bungalows, shops, roads, trees, and all the civilization that time and a great expenditure can alone produce. The barracks of the English troops occupied a line of great extent, fronting a noble parade ground, cleared from every impediment to the movement of men. The headquarters of the Bengal Artillery were on the right; the Rifles in the infantry barracks were in the centre; and the 6th Dragoon Guards (*carabiniers*) in the cavalry barracks on the left.

The military stations in India are on the plan of a camp. The lines occupied by the men face to the clear and open country; next come the hospital, cook-houses, gymnasia, canteens, and other buildings; and then the houses of the officers. To the rear of these in Meerut was a magnificent road termed the Mall, and behind that the space was filled up by numerous houses and *bazaars*. The only enclosed buildings were the Dum-Dum and the General Hospital; the former behind the artillery, containing stores for that branch of the service; and the latter in rear of the infantry. A wide space separated the artillery and infantry from the cavalry, who occupied a long range of handsome barracks just completed.

The native lines faced to the left of those held by the English troops, commencing about a mile or so to their rear. They were very commodious, having been built for seven battalions. The long rows of bungalows for the officers of these battalions, each surrounded by its compound, were separated from the chief or *Suddur bazaar* only by a street. This *bazaar*, in 1857, had more pretensions to be called a city than many of the most populous towns of India. If lines were drawn at right-angles from the right of the European and from the left of the native barracks to the rear, at the point where they met, the square would be complete; and all that space containing many thousands of acres was crowded with the residences of civil and military function-aries, citizens, public buildings, and *bazaars*. The whole was shaded by the foliage of well-grown trees, and intersected with numerous and beautifully constructed roads.

The walled city that gives its name to the station lies a short way behind the *Suddur bazaar*.

The great cantonment was built with no more regard to defence than Cheltenham or Manchester. Our maxim was that we must beat our enemy in the open field, or wherever he might be entrenched, or cease to rule in India. Armies had gone forth from Meerut to conquer provinces—no one dreamt that the time would come when we should there, tremble for our lives. One of the objects for which the spot was selected was to overawe the Imperial city of Delhi, distant about thirty-five miles by a good road. It was not imagined that the turn of events could reverse this order, and that the period would arrive when the Imperial city would overawe the military station.

The troops passed through the *bazaars*, driving the *Goojurs* from the gardens of the houses. In the streets not a human being was to be seen, though half-an-hour before they were filled with the predatory tribes for which, in former years, this neighbourhood was notorious.

A few mangled victims were taken from the ditches and the force bivouacked on the Mall, throwing a chain of sentries around their lines. So continuous was the musketry in the *bazaars* that it seemed as if a great action were going on; and amidst the cries of the frantic *Goojurs* and the blaze of the houses around, I venture to say that few slept that night within miles of the circle of Meerut.

The conduct of the *sepoys* in avoiding the battle here offered damped the ardour of their Meerut partisans. They had boasted everywhere that they were more than a match for the European garrison; yet they fled, scarcely firing a shot not discharged at an unarmed man.

At dawn the brigade again marched on the native lines, seeking out the enemy, whose course was not yet known, but at that time the *sowars* were riding into the city of Delhi. Far over the clear and level parade ground a crowd of *Goojurs* hung like a cloud, and a similar body could be traced during the day in the neighbourhood of the European lines. For some time, these men waited the evacuation of Meerut, or the destruction of the English, for on this they seem with confidence to have calculated.

They were soon to learn the nature of the champion they had backed, and that those who intend to prey on British spoil must act with courage, and nerve every sinew for the enterprise. From amidst the yet smoking ruins of the houses, from the streets and from ditches, the remains of the murdered were taken; and with horror the officers saw the mangled bodies, scarcely to be distinguished, of ladies they knew well, lying naked on the ground, hacked with sabres. The soldiers picked up their comrades. The men spoke little; there was no outburst of feeling, though in their hearts was seared the memory of the scene.

Though I shrink from details, yet a sketch is necessary, for the horrible character of the outbreak is not fully understood in England. Frequently I have been asked if the reported murders and escapes were true, and even if any foundation existed for such reports. In the first instance, as usual, the nation exaggerated the crimes of the rebellion, and ended, in the reaction sure to follow, by disbelieving plain and true statements. To such a result tended the accounts of men who saw the retribution, but not the provocation; who beheld the cringing figure and clasped hands of the wretch mercilessly consigned to the gallows—but not the yelling fiend with dripping sword and hands red with blood, mutilating the bodies of those who had never injured him.

I will take the first house, because a true type of what numbers

DEATH OF COLONEL FINNIS AT MEERUT
(The outbreak of the Mutiny on 10th May, 1857)

throughout India were destined to become; and one spot of roadside, which furnished but a poor sample of many more terrible scenes.

Near the gaol stood a neat brick *chunammed* bungalow. This gaol held the *sowars*, whose sentence of imprisonment had precipitated the revolt. It was situated behind the lines of their corps, and the first act of the Third Cavalry, who led the revolt, was to release their comrades and the other convicts in confinement.

It was Sunday evening and, I believe, a few friends had assembled in this house. They must have been surrounded and every hope of escape lost before even a conception of what was impending had entered their minds. The conclusions Colonel Muter formed were from what he saw. It seemed that they had fled to their bed and bathrooms, seeking any hiding-place in their desperate extremity.

Attempts had been made to burn down the bungalow, which were defeated by the nature of the materials, and the volumes of smoke had only blackened the walls and the ceilings, as if to throw a pall over the tragic acts the fire refused to obliterate, leaving the place a charnel-house black with crime. The doors and window-frames had been torn from their positions, the furniture was gone, the matting in shreds and trampled by a thousand feet, the plaster soiled and broken.

Following in the flight of the inmates a bedroom was entered, where a pile in the centre attracted attention, requiring inspection to understand what it was. The proceedings, of which the proofs lay here, were difficult to realise, and took some time to comprehend. Men and women dying from sword-cut wounds must have been heaped upon their own broken furniture, till the vestiges left by the fire applied to the pile did not even tell the number of the victims.

The walls were dark with smoke, the floor stained with blood, and the air tainted with the smell. It was easy to trace the rush of desperate men into the small adjoining apartments, where their bodies lay just as they had furnished subjects for the brave swords of the rabble to hack at and to hew. However sad may be the look of a soldier on the field after an action, there is no horror in the gaze of the dead who fell fairly with arms in their hands and the excitement of battle in their hearts. But it shocks even the sternest to see men murdered by their bedsides, and still more to see women. Before the frenzy of excess that suggested and carried out the funeral pile the soldier stood aghast; and an impression was produced perhaps never afterwards erased.

A little way from this spot two riflemen of my husband's company lay on the road in such a state that none save their own comrades could recognise them. On the evening preceding the Mutiny they had received an advance of pay with a furlough and were bound to the hills in a government bullock van, when they were attacked by the mob, the first in the attack being their driver. The body of a lady lay in a ditch on the other side of a slight embankment, so disfigured by wounds as to be with difficulty recognised. A track was discernible along the duct of the road from the *bazaar* to the place, showing clearly, she had been dragged over the ground and thrown where she lay. The corpse of another murdered woman was in the same ditch a little beyond.

But why follow these details? Why wonder that our country people cannot comprehend the full barbarity of these unprovoked massacres, when those who saw them recall the scenes more as a dream than as a reality—an enduring impression left by a hideous vision? This *bazaar* was only three or four hours in the hands of the mutineers; and as my mind wanders from cantonment to cantonment that fell wholly into their possession, a shifting scene of horror goes by, which I know only faintly portrays the facts.

It was probable the Mutiny would begin at a station held by European troops, from the fact that these only had the commanders possessing the power to coerce; and so, it proved, for it was in the attempt to punish the mutinous conduct of the 3rd (Native) Cavalry that the revolt was precipitated. How much we owe to this precipitation may be best conjectured by considering the plan said to have been prepared by the *sepoys*. On the queen's birthday, which was to be celebrated one fortnight later, they were to parade according to their plot, with arms loaded and pouches filled with ball-cartridge. It was then the custom for British regiments to stand by the side of Indian battalions and fire a *feu-de-joie* in honour of the event. The captain of each company of Europeans then saw the service ammunition carefully removed, and its place supplied by three rounds of blank. While the English soldier was discharging his harmless powder in the air, the bullets of his Hindoo ally were to be directed to his heart.

The scheme was simple and practicable in the highest degree, and if carried out with secrecy and resolution, would have swept every European solider in one and the same hour from the face of India. A massacre more foul, more widespread, more disastrous, had never before been in the power of a people. Had it been carried out, Her Majesty would have had the heartrending reflection that her birthday was the blackest in the annals of a nation whose history extends over a thousand years, and whose operations embrace the globe. If ever in human events the hand of God has been manifest it was displayed during this perilous period. From the beginning of the outbreak to the fall of Delhi our career was a succession of miraculous deliverances; and perhaps there was no officer of experience and intelligence in the country who would have considered our escape possible, in the event of a general mutiny of the Bengal Army, had that opinion been asked, before the Mutiny began.

It is noteworthy that a minor but most important detail worked for our preservation on that eventful Sunday evening. In consequence of the increasing heat of the season, the hour for the service in the church had that day been ordered a half hour later. Had the battalion marched at the usual time, they would have been in the church and unarmed, an easy prey to the mutineers, who calculated on this position; whereas the 60th had not assembled, and to their surprise and consternation the mutineers saw the battalion marching down to their lines armed and fully accoutred for action.

General Hewitt, who commanded the Meerut Division, had been trained in a native regiment. One of the points of such training was to place the utmost confidence in the valour and fidelity of the *sepoys*. The officers boasted that these battalions had broken French regiments in fair and open fight, and had advanced in the face of dangers where even British troops had flinched. The effects of this teaching were seen when the Mutiny commenced. The officers of the regiments which had not yet mutinied pledged their lives on the fidelity of their men, and many fell victims to the noble feeling of reliance nothing could shake. These officers, with the same confidence, would have led their men against any enemy. It was not fair to expect the general to act in direct contradiction to this feeling, so carefully fostered by the nation itself.

The native garrison, consisting of the 11th and 20th Bengal Infantry and the 3rd Cavalry, were about equal in numbers to the European soldiers. These men openly bragged of the courage for which they had been lauded in the despatches of a century, with all a native's hectoring. The people around believed in them. They were aided by tens of thousands of *Goojurs* and of camp followers. The three regiments rose suddenly on the station—unprepared—with arms in their hands and ammunition in their pouches. The surprise is that so little, not that so much was effected.

It is impossible to tell what the result would have been had they marched immediately on the European lines, or even defended their own against our attack—as was done with so fatal an effect at Jhelum. The first course might have been destruction, the last must have been disastrous to us; for the *sepoys* were in a position to bear a heavy loss, while each European soldier killed was a direct step towards their goal.

Blame has been showered on the Meerut garrison for not pursuing the mutineers to Delhi. Leaving the existing circumstances out of consideration, the cantonment itself had to be safeguarded, being filled with *Goojurs* and *badmashes* intent on violence and plunder. The *carabiniers*, on whom the pursuit would have devolved, had recently arrived, and consisted chiefly of recruits who could not ride, on horses not yet trained to carry a rider. The heat was that of a furnace, and to proceed in a pursuit of an acclimatised native cavalry regiment, mounted on trained horses, which would be received, housed, and fed at the end of their thirty miles' journey, would have been foolhardy in the extreme. With the European cavalry it is terrible to think what their sufferings would unavoidably have been, without commissariat, without even water for men or horses. Any serious check at the commencement would have been ruinous to us. Might not such a check have followed the despatch of a few hundreds of men to a city filled with fanatics, and in the hands of a revolted garrison, consisting of regiments of all arms, complete in every appointment?

The officer who had first to test the real value of these regiments, where such great interests hung on the result, might well pause to gather around him every element of strength. Subsequent events showed that the *sepoy* had been overrated—that he ceased to be formidable when deprived of his English officers. Without them he was a tiger with his teeth extracted and his claws pared; and no answer could be more complete than this to the abuse so often heaped on our military officers.

The English officer has led the battalions of Portugal to beat those of France, and the hordes of Turkey to repulse the regiments of Russia; he has shed on this Hindoo Army a century of renown, and in the most isolated positions, supported by courage and strength of character, he has bent and swayed the wild tribes around, directing by force of will their untrained energies and valour into channels useful to his country; but by far the greatest of his exploits has been the conquest and fame his leadership has extracted from materials so worthless as this Hindoo Army.

I believe that the Mutiny could not have been checked by the

European garrison of Meerut, and that the immediate employment of this force in its suppression would have led to the most serious disasters. It was not a local disturbance, but one planned with elaboration throughout the country.

CHAPTER 2

The first feeling at Meerut was akin to despair. The small body of British knew that they would be opposed to the whole Bengal army, in possession of immense magazines and stores, and from the savage manner the *Goojurs*, as well as camp followers, had handled the stragglers they met, the idea was that millions of natives would be in insurrection around.

Those unacquainted with the climate of the North-West Provinces in May and June can form no conception of the task that fell to our countrymen. It was supposed to be impossible for us during these months to exist under canvas; and this opinion was calculated on by the *sepoys* when planning the outbreak. Stringent orders were in force against exposure from a short period after sunrise until sunset; but notwithstanding every care and excellent barrack accommodation, many annually died from excessive heat.

It was with no feelings of surprise that the tidings were received of the rise at Delhi, and the massacre of the Christian community. It will be an open question for history whether those massacres could have been prevented by any move of the Meerut garrison. The general and the brigadier were much blamed at the time; and I think with as much reason as a well-found ship struggling in a hurricane might be blamed for looking on at an ill-found vessel overwhelmed by the same blast, without making a useless as well as dangerous attempt to save the crew.

If a march on the Imperial city would have been a false move, endangering the Empire, the Christian community could not thus have been saved. Even had that move been made and been a success, it is doubtful whether it would have saved these people. All the arguments hinge on the supposition that the Native Army would not have fought—a supposition in direct opposition to facts. For the same reason that the regiments at Meerut rose to save their comrades from imprisonment, the regiments at Delhi would rise to save them from the gallows.

The following circumstance precipitated the Mutiny at Meerut. On May 5th cartridges of the old kind, which they and their fathers had used, were served out to the 3rd (Native) Cavalry, when eighty-five men at once stepped out and refused to take them. The men were confined, brought to a court-martial composed of native officers, and by those native officers condemned to periods of imprisonment with hard labour varying from six to ten years.

General Hewitt then prepared to carry out the sentences. The mutineers were placed under a European guard composed of two companies of the 60th Rifles and twenty-five men of the 6th Dragoon Guards, and a general parade was ordered for the morning of May 9th. At daybreak on that Saturday morning all the troops in the station, leaving the guards standing, paraded on the 60th parade ground; the *carabiniers*, the 60th Rifles, the 3rd Light Cavalry (Natives), the 11th and 20th Native Infantry, a light field battery, and a troop of Horse Artillery. The *carabiniers* and the Rifles were then ordered to load and be ready, and the horse artillery the same. This done, the mutineers were marched on the ground, the European troops and the artillery guns being so placed that the least movement of disaffection would have been followed by instant slaughter.

The mutineers were in uniform when marched in; they were stripped of clothes and accoutrements, and the armourer's and smith's departments of the horse artillery being in readiness, every man was ironed and shackled for ten years' imprisonment on the hard roads with the exception of five, whose period was limited to six years. After appealing in vain for mercy, the prisoners reproached their comrades of the 3rd Cavalry for permitting the sentence to be carried out. It was afterwards known that an understanding existed between the culprits and the native soldiery, who had sworn that the sentence should never be carried into effect. No thought of the need of a European guard ever suggested itself, so the prisoners were handed over to the civil authorities and lodged in the gaol some two miles distant and placed under native warders.

The native soldiers returned to their lines in the greatest excitement, and, it is said, immediately not only planned the outbreak that took place the following day, but sent word to the regiments in Delhi of their intention to rise and to be ready to receive them on their arrival at Delhi.

So complete and so secret were their plans that Mr. Greathed, the commissioner, to whom all looked for the first intimation of danger, was wholly unaware of the proceedings, and therefore was unable to give a hint to the military. This has always appeared to me surprising, as for many months a feeling of unrest had existed among the Hindoos, a feeling that should not have been overlooked or minimised. Rumours had been widely spread that the government intended to force Christianity upon them, and that this was to be done through the suppression of the system of caste, which could be best and most insidiously done by means of the greased cartridge for the Enfield rifle recently introduced to supplant the old "Brown Bess."

In Appendix (Vol. I., of Kaye's excellent *History of the Sepoy War*) we find the following interesting original orders drawn up by the Military Board in 1847 and approved by the commander-in-chief and the governor-general:—

1. The ammunition of the two-grooved rifles is to be prepared as blank cartridge of three drachms of musketry powder, in blue paper, made up in bundles of ten.

2. The balls to be put up, five in a string, in small cloth bags with a greased patch of fine cloth—a portion carried in a ballbag attached to the girdle on the right side, and the remainder in pouch.

3. Patches to be made of calico or long-cloth and issued ready greased from magazines; a portion of the greasing composition will also be issued with the patches for the purpose of renewal when required, and instructions for its preparation forwarded to magazine officers by the Military Board.

The following were the instructions issued:—

The mode of preparing the grease and applying it to the cloth to be as follows: To three pints of country linseed oil, add one-fourth of a pound of beeswax, which mix by melting the wax in a ladle, pouring the oil in and allowing it to remain on the fire until the composition is thoroughly melted. The cloth is then to be dipped in it until every part is saturated, and held by one corner until the mixture ceases to run, after which it is to be laid out as smoothly as possible on a clean spot to cool. The above quantity of composition will answer for three yards of long-cloth, from which 1,200 patches can be made.

These instructions were approved by the governor-general, Lord Hardinge, in a letter from the military secretary to the adjutant-general, dated April 6th, 1847, and no subsequent cancelling order can be traced. On the contrary, the officer who held the post of Inspector of Ordnance during Lord Dalhousie's Administration, assured the historian that this composition continued in use up to 1857, so that it seems that the impression that the patches were greased with animal fat must have been erroneous. It is clear, from the disastrous results of such an idea, that the widest publicity should have been given to the true nature of the materials used, and every effort made to meet and remove all doubt; for the more the origin of the uprising is studied, the more evident it appears that the movement on the part of the *sepoys* was more a revolt—with much of panic in it—against a suspected attack on their religion and caste, than as we all at first thought, a struggle for Empire.

It has often been said that the sight of a body of dragoons crossing the bridge of boats would have changed the aspect of affairs, cowed the city, and quelled the mutinous spirit. It is a pity that the whole force of these dragoons, backed by the artillery and the Rifles—whose bullets afterwards told with such deadly effect—could not suppress the insurrection at the spot where it originated. This argument renders Euclid's axiom thus: "*A part is greater than the whole*," and makes it when so put of double force, as the *sepoys* at Delhi were increased threefold, while our strength would have been diminished at least in that ratio, if we had despatched a force in pursuit—comparing the detachment with the Meerut garrison.

I believe that the dust raised by the dragoons would have been the signal for the massacre of every Christian in Delhi, and for a strife that might have ended in the massacre of every Christian in these provinces. And in this I am also borne out by the occurrences in Meerut. The *sepoys*, the camp followers, the *Goojurs*, hastened to kill when they rose; and though the English garrison was only a mile distant, its people could not be saved whom the mob had surrounded. With their fate before us, can it be supposed that the Christians, entangled in the most fanatical city in India, encompassed by walls, could have been preserved by a portion of that garrison, thirty-five miles off, who had failed in this very object in their own cantonment? If the insurgent *sepoys* from Meerut had found the road barred and had taken another direction, it is clear the English in Delhi would have been in a similar position as those at Cawnpore or at Bareilly, and perhaps even fewer might have eventually escaped. The intelligence of the rise at Meerut at once made mutineers of all native garrisons.

The subsequent history of every station in Bengal, where no European troops were quartered, was the record of an attempt to avert or delay the catastrophe, ending in a ride for life and a massacre. It cannot be supposed that the garrison would not be affected by the news, stationed as it was in the very focus whence the treason emanated. Sooner or later this portion of the native soldiery was sure to rise, and the fanatical and disaffected citizens even more certain still—whether or not, a mutineer from Meerut had entered the capital of the emperor.

Within that fortified city was our greatest arsenal. Its name touches a chord in the Mussulman's heart, and its history gives it a political importance which neither its wealth nor population warrants. It was natural that the Mutiny should gather to a head in this strong city—strong in the moral power which the possession of the recognised capital of India gives—stronger still with the representative of the ancient emperors supporting the revolt from the seat where his ancestors had for centuries governed the empire, and stronger yet in all the materials of war.

As the native regiments poured into Delhi the British residents in Meerut left their houses and concentrated in the infantry and artillery lines, abandoning the barracks of the cavalry; and thus, the whole force was grouped within a small circle. The Dum-Dum and the General Hospital were fortified; *chevaux-de-frise* bristled in front, and from embrasures the mouths of cannon menaced the surrounding country.

Within, the circle was full of life; officers and men lounged about, horses were picketed in long rows, guards held every post, sentries challenged in all directions, and gangs of coolies were constantly at work.

Outside this busy ring the country wore the most miserable aspect. The gardens around the desolate houses were hastening to decay; nothing stirred on the roads once so gay with life; here and there the blackened walls of a bungalow, destroyed on the tenth, stood drearily up; but the scene of the great ruin was in the native lines. There, streets of houses had been consumed; and it is impossible to convey a just idea of its sadness. The charred rafters, the black walls, the broken carriage resting on a half-burnt wheel, the skeleton of a bullock lying on a bed of withered flowers—dead, for want of the water it once drew; the blasted trees, scorched in the great fire—all combined, with the recollection of the fate of the inhabitants, to form a picture so painfully desolate that the spot was rarely visited.

The *bazaars* were silent as if depopulated by a plague; scarcely a native was to be seen. Trade had ceased; the telegraph-wire lay cut on the ground, and the poles were rotting by its side—no means of communication existed. Even the peasant ceased to cultivate, and it became difficult to believe that the district was one of the best tilled and the most populous in the world.

At night all this was strangely changed. The ceaseless boom of powder ignited in *chatties* sounded like cannon from the surrounding villages; the horizon was lit up by great fires, and officers speculated as they gazed at the glare of a distant flame on what village or town was being destroyed. Without intermission the sound of musketry continued from the neighbouring *bazaars* to warn off murderers and robbers who stalked abroad. Even within a short distance of our fortifications, a party who rode into a village found the inhabitants lying dead in the streets, and some women and children weeping over the bodies of their kindred.

So, this province that knew war only by tradition, or by the accounts of far-off battles—where even an execution was rare—became at once steeped in blood. Fire ran over the land, wholesale murder shocked mankind, and pillage and revenge took the place of law. It may be that the natural bent of the people, repressed by the hand of power, rebounded with violence when that pressure was removed. Men that could not be roused to patriotism rose to rapine; village wreaked its hoarded vengeance on village; man, on man. The cruel Asiatic, in his frenzy, spared neither women nor children; and when these were the wives and little ones of his Saxon ruler, he struck a blow that stirred the deep heart of that master.

How far the people were really hostile we could not then ascertain, but it was clear that there was a large element in the population that eagerly seized the opportunity to give scope to their lawless instincts.

Some weeks previous to the outbreak I had noticed, when giving orders for dinner and telling what guests were expected, that the *khansamah* who had to carry out my instructions was unusually sorrowful, and at last I remarked, "I do not wish to intrude into your affairs, but I perceive something is distressing you, and if it is anything in which I can assist you let me know."

He then told me with tears he was troubled about his only son who had a severe malady in one of his legs. He had tried all remedies, and native doctors had at last given up the case.

"We will see what we can do," I said, and thereupon wrote a note to our clever surgeon, Sir John Ker-Innes, telling the *khansamah* to take it himself, and to explain the symptoms. Sir John instantly came, saw the boy, ordered a plaister from the hospital of the 60th entirely to encase the leg, directed that it should not be touched for ten days, and then must not be removed except under his superintendence. At the expiration of that time Sir John Innes came, ordered the plaister to be removed with the result—a perfect cure! The father rushed into the house, not to tell, but to *worship me!* I told him I would leave the room, that all I had done was to invite a very clever surgeon to exert his talents to cure his child, and even that would not have availed, had not *Allah* blessed the steps taken.

Nothing, however, could disturb the impression on the *khansamah's* mind that I had exerted a saintly influence in the case, and my *ayah* told me I was perfectly safe, in the anxious days still before us, for the *khansamah*, a bigoted Mussulman, had undertaken to watch over me when I returned to our house, and Colonel Muter was absent on duty. As soon as it became dark, he would conceal himself for the whole night among the trees of our garden, keeping close scrutiny on my doors.

Besides the families who had forsaken their houses the refugees from the district assembled in the Dum-Dum, and the life it then presented was new to us all. The principal buildings were three long barracks, and the families were there grouped together during the day—the ladies at work and the children at play—eating at long tables, and living more in public than accords with English tastes. Every available spot was covered with a tent, where the nights were passed; some held the guards of the Dum-Dum, and the wife of a judge, and the soldier on duty were placed in close proximity.

Terrible stories circulated freely in these barrack-rooms, for the thoughts of all were centred in one great object, and the eager anxiety for news rose almost to a mania. Manufacturers of *gup*, (gossip), as it was termed, had a lively time, and imagination was freely called into play; yet imagination and fiction, with every advantage, were beaten by the truth, for I remember no story, however horrible, that equalled the realities of Cawnpore.

The first rumours related to the march of the Sappers from the engineer station of Roorkee, and that of Major Reid's regiment of Goorkhas from Deyhra Dhoon. Great doubts were expressed regarding the fidelity of the former. First it was reported they had killed their officers and marched for Delhi; next they were depicted as filled with horror at the conduct of the cavalry and infantry; but the strangest course was that they actually took, for they marched into Meerut only to murder their commander, and many of them to fall under the sabres of the 6th Dragoon Guards. The true and gallant conduct of Major Reid's Goorkhas, now historical, was even then scarcely doubted.

Among the fugitives were many who had escaped the massacre at

Delhi. Tender women who had sprung down the fortifications amid a storm of bullets—who had waded through rapid rivers, and walked under a sun whose scorching rays cannot be known save by those who have felt them—stealing along paths occupied by a hostile population. What heroism, what endurance, what hair-breadth escapes! These plain narratives contained examples to nerve men's hearts for the terrible strife before them, and, if needs be, to show us all how to die with fortitude.

The surgeon had given me some rooms in the Rifle hospital until wanted for sick and wounded soldiers, and our servants and some furniture were moved to this asylum. These buildings were not so extensively fortified as the Dum-Dum, but the rooms were filled with the sick who were armed and, however ill, would turn out to fight if the necessity arose. I was thankful for the security, as my husband was constantly engaged on duty, a third of the battalion being required each night to rest on their arms on the Mall. My life here was much more quiet than in the Dum-Dum, though it was less sustained by companionship and the exciting tales there constantly afloat.

The news of the Mutiny spread through India like wildfire, and reached the commander-in-chief at Simla. Instantly the three regiments in the hills were ordered to Umballa, and the Delhi Field Force rapidly assembled there, under the personal command of General Anson. For a brief period, the communication with Agra by telegraph was restored, and the general received his instructions to detach a large portion of his force to join the commander-in-chief and to proclaim martial law in the district. Then the waves of the rebellion surged over the country, and left Meerut like a rock isolated in a sea of trouble.

However, martial law had already been proclaimed, and Meerut had tasted of the bitterness felt by the English, and infused into their acts by the proceedings I have described. A gallows had been erected not far from the burial ground where lay the victims of the Meerut massacre. The first to suffer was a butcher who had taken the most active part in the murder of a lady; he had been captured gallantly by an officer, and was hanged by order of the general.

The most ferocious who had assisted in the fire and bloodshed that had desolated the station were to be found among our own camp followers. The butchers led, and it is said the tailors strove to vie with them; then came masons, carpenters, bakers and all the rabble who had rushed into the streets on that fatal evening to destroy the unarmed soldier in his afternoon stroll. The butchers followed the *sepoys* to Delhi and perhaps took part in the crimes there perpetrated.

When this engrossing pursuit ended, they returned to Meerut to resume their avocations, where they were seized and compelled to undergo an ordeal which blanched the cheeks and shook the limbs of many who had been loudest in cry and foremost in cruelty and exposed them to each other as the cowardly ruffians they were. It was difficult to obtain evidence, and they were sent round the garrison, drawn up in a row; while company after company and troop after troop was halted before them, and the men asked if they could recognise any of the number as having been engaged in the riots. Most of their faces wore a deadly hue—some could scarcely stand and all their lips muttered prayers, the name of *Allah* alone being distinguishable.

The natives condemned to death generally assumed a stoical indifference and moved with composure to the place of execution, sometimes picking their way over ground wet with heavy showers as if more concerned for their health than for their fate. It was then, and then only, in this terrible trial, they displayed any nobility of spirit.

In compliance with these orders from Agra, a wing of the 60th, a wing of the *carabiniers* and a strong force of artillery marched for Delhi on May 25th, and Colonel Muter was left in command of the wing of his regiment that remained. As he, with the few officers present, was required to sleep where the men lay on their arms, I was left much alone.

The fatal results of war were soon brought to our door. In a few days the column was met on the Hindun by a native force from Delhi, when the test regarded by many with so much anxiety was tried. Here, for the first time, British regiments met our *sepoy* regiments as deadly enemies. The ground was chosen by the natives, and heavy artillery was most judiciously placed; but after a sharp action that artillery was captured and the enemy was driven back into the city. On the following day a second division drew across the road to dispute the passage of the column; they also were driven in confusion over the river, and the king heard in his palace the roar of the guns and saw the men who boasted that on their arms rested the empire, broken like sheep by the master-hand that had taught them to conquer.

Doolies (light palanquin for carrying the sick) containing wounded men came back to the hospital, and amongst them a gallant young officer who had left us in high health and spirits, and whose life was now ebbing fast. Poor Napier was buried in the graveyard at Meerut, one of the earliest victims in battle of a war destined to swallow up a host. In that cemetery lie the victims of the first massacre, and near the bridge of the Hindun, to the right, as the traveller passes to Delhi, a mound covers the remains of those who first fell in the field.

Under it rests Captain Andrews, to whom I had just bid *adieu*. He was killed at the head of a party of his men, after the capture of the guns, by the explosion of an ammunition waggon, and one of the worst cases among the wounded was that of a soldier who was standing near him at the time. This man had been picked up more like a cinder than a human being, yet, by care, he recovered; and it was a pleasure for me to supply to him and other brave men many little delicacies permitted by the doctors.

The column passed up the Jumna and crossed by a bridge of boats some twelve miles above the city, where they joined the Field Force. Not long after, this bridge was destroyed, and the left bank of the river fell into the possession of the rebels.

On June 8th the field force moved on Delhi; and at Badli-ka-Serai, some three miles outside the walls, they found the enemy in position. After a well-contested action, the *sepoys* were defeated for the third time, with the loss of their guns, and pursued to the walls of their stronghold. Then commenced a siege that will live long in history—a siege on which hung greater interests than on any other undertaken by our country, and the memory of which will last, a monument of the endurance and courage of the British soldier.

CHAPTER 3

When the detachment from our garrison had crossed the river, the road became clear and open between the rapidly increasing force of the mutineers and our cantonment. The spies of the "Intelligence Department" now constantly brought reports of the preparations at Delhi for the attack on Meerut. These accounts gave full particulars of the *durbars* held, the regiments ordered, the guns detailed, and the king's commands to the chief who was to direct the expedition. Spies were taken by us measuring the ditch, noting the guns, and our means of defence, and all held it was more than probable the attack would be attempted.

Immense preparations were made to repel the threatened assault; enormous fortifications arose around the Infantry barracks, enclosing the houses of the officers. Roads were cut across; the trees and mud walls of the compounds were cleared away from the front of the guns; masses of grain were stored; and a position was selected and strengthened on the open plain to meet the rebels on the march.

The extensive nature of these works imposed on the country, covered the real weakness of the position, and cowed the followers of the *mogul*, who could find no general to command or troops to undertake a service attended with so much danger.

A few lighted arrows fired into the thatched roofs of our barracks would have burnt us all out, and left us exposed to the deadly rays of the sun. But the mutineers had broken away from all discipline and control, and given themselves up to riot and plunder, and from the capital, thronged with well-armed and trained soldiers, scarcely an enterprise demanding courage and vigour was undertaken. The entire district was left to us; expeditions were constantly going forth from Meerut, and the severe and summary punishment inflicted on the insurgent villages kept in awe the unruly tribes of *Goojurs* around.

The tales of murder at Moradabad, at Bareilly, at Agra, at Lucknow, of mutiny in the camp, of treachery, even within our fortifications, kept us in a constant thrill of alarm. Now I heard of the overwhelming force of the rebels at Delhi; the death of the commander-in-chief, the hopelessness of the siege, of the capture of Calcutta; then dim rumours of Cawnpore, of the rise of Oude and Rohilcund, of the murder of Sir John Lawrence, and the insurrection in the Punjaub. Truth was strangely mixed with fable; some of the reports were wholly true, and most founded on probabilities. The real ignorance of events was harassing in the extreme, as our fate depended as much on circumstances occurring at extremities of the country, of which we could gain no tidings, as on those that more nearly concerned us.

In all our hearts was a painful anxiety how the news from India would be viewed in England. On that rested our ultimate preservation. If the nation, alive to the great emergency, put forth her mighty strength, we should be saved; if not, the chances were—we died. Month passed away after month, and the anxious desire for news from home grew in intensity. That Delhi should fall; that our country should rise in wrath and deliver India, were the daily prayers offered up by the British community, now fairly at bay throughout these provinces.

When the sun had set the people assembled in the Dum-Dum in a circle, and the chaplain—the Rev. J. E. Wharton Rotton—repeated prayers and portions of Scripture, his extraordinary memory enabling him to do this without a book. That concluded the day, and nothing was afterwards heard save the call of the sentries repeating, from post to post, the cry, "All's well!"

My *khansamah*, a bigoted Mussulman, became troublesome as the

GROUP OF OFFICERS (60TH) TAKEN IMMEDIATELY AFTER THE SIEGE
by Sir John Ker-Innes, K.C.B. (Much marred)

Sir John Jones, K.C.B., in Centre; The Rev. J. E. Wharton Rotton,
Chaplain to "Delhi Field Force," immediately behind him

Mutiny progressed. He entered with interest into the rumours current in the *bazaars*, and retailed them to his fellow-servants in the worst light.

When transacting his market business with me he often inquired about the news from Agra, whither he seemed to turn most hopefully, and sometimes he ventured the remark that there was very bad news from that city. At the worst time of the siege of Delhi he earnestly applied for a few days' leave, which I granted; and I was afterwards informed he employed the period in visiting the besieged city, and inspecting its means of defence, as well as the character of the operations directed against it. I noticed a change in his manner on his return, as if the piles of artillery, the pyramids of shot, and the racks of the great arsenal, filled up to the ceiling with small arms, had inspired him with confidence, and he could foresee the approach of Mussulman ascendency, when *Allah's* name would resound over the land, and the followers of Mahomet alone be considered eligible for the loaves and fishes.

Among a people who find it difficult to tell a true tale, the stories circulated were more false than those in our circle. The wildest rumours gained ready credence with the natives, and they firmly believed our power in India was at an end. The *ayah*, who looked on the Mutiny with dread, would come full of a tale of extermination she had obtained from the *khansamah*, and I was obliged to warn him that his conduct might lead to serious consequences to himself. The *ayah* regarded the revolt from a professional point of view.

"Who will give us bread," she asked, "when the ladies and children are murdered or driven from the land?" She had heard that before the English came, natives of her class feared to wear good clothes, or to show signs of comfort, for such display led to extortion by the followers of the *rajahs* and from *nawabs* in whose districts they lived; and I am persuaded the truth of this was felt by numbers of the lower classes. I was able to speak in Hindustani sufficiently to ask for anything in common use, but not to converse in that language either fluently or grammatically. Yet I could understand much more than I could speak, and would listen with interest to all this native woman had to say relative to her country and people. Sometimes she would peep into the room where I was sitting and, disregarding my preoccupation, glide in, squat on the floor at my feet, and look up with a smile.

"Now, what is it, *ayah?*" I would ask.

"Want to talk to *Mem-Sahib*," she would reply.

"Not now; do you not see I am busy?"

"Never mind, do that tomorrow"—and who could resist her handsome, loving, happy-looking face?

In these talks, I also gained much intimate knowledge of the people. I became more and more convinced that this was a *sepoy* revolt against what they feared was an attack on their caste and religion. The Mahomedans saw in its success a chance for the King of Delhi to regain power; and there are always in India vast tribes of thieves and unrestrained ruffians who, under the names of *Goojurs* and *badmashes*, are ready for riot, murder, and plunder at any period of anarchy and general unrest. The country, as a whole, was not against us; therefore, I consider it a misnomer to style it the "Indian Mutiny," when "*Sepoy Revolt*" is by far the more correct appellation.

From whatever cause, there can now be little question of the general fidelity of our servants during this trying period. Gentlemen speak in terms of high praise of the conduct of the *syces*—always close to their master's horse even under fire; of the water-carriers, *dooly*-bearers, and others, besides the house servants, many of whom fell in the campaigns. Our Mussulman watercarriers, however, left us during the gloomiest period to return to Moradabad, then in the hands of the rebels, though much kindness had been shown to both, who were father and son.

It is certain that the assumption of power and confidence on the part of the English, greatly swayed the natives with whom they came in contact, and much contributed to the defeat of the revolt. The people were treated with extreme harshness and the servants often met with bad usage. The good and evil qualities of our race told alike in our favour in the emergency. The courage and vigour and haughtiness and stubborn pride, the insolence and even the cruelty, half disdainful, half revengeful, all spread their influence around, and individual men thus upheld in whole districts the prestige of our rule. Not one act of revolt was committed by the people of Meerut after May 10th; and although numbers were executed, no signs of disaffection were shown.

Among those who sought protection within our fortified circle were the nuns of the Convent of Sirdhana, a pretty place about ten miles from Meerut, the property of the late Dyce Sombre. Apartments in the hospital had been allotted to them, and I visited the Lady Superior. I was much struck with the beauty of one of the Sisters, Madame St. Anthony. She gave me an account of the mutiny at Sirdhana, of the tumultuous gathering of the natives, and the way they threatened the convent. A man from the town offered them protection for one hundred and fifty *rupees*. While the Lady Superior was considering, another came forward with a similar demand. As such negotiation was fruitless, the ladies determined to trust alone in Providence. Calculating that plunder would be the chief object, they all assembled on the flat roof of the large building, and taking only the Host with them, they awaited the result, when they were relieved by a party of volunteers from Meerut.

On my expressing sympathy for their alarm, she said with a placid smile: "No alarm was felt, for they were prepared."

However strongly her mind and her faith may have sustained her, she was physically unequal to such shocks, and I was deeply grieved a few weeks later to hear of her untimely death.

But these were times when death was in many instances a blessing. The very air of India was charged with horrors. The weary watching, the sickening expectation, and the wearing effects of the climate had a depressing tendency that required much resolution to struggle against, and all the consolations of religion to sustain. The men were relieved by action, but for the women there was not this resource. The Roman Catholic priests of Meerut directed the members of their church to repeat the seventy-ninth Psalm with their daily devotions, and we all sympathised in heart and spirit not only with that, and the forty-sixth Psalm, but with all the promises of protection and blessing in answer to earnest prayer contained in the Book of Books.

A regiment of Seikhs was detached to Meerut and two hundred of the 60th, one hundred artillerymen, and the wounded who had recovered were directed to join the camp before Delhi, and on the night of August 26th my husband left me, to command this party of his regiment.

I will not attempt to enlarge on my feelings during this unhappy period of my life.

When the fortifications had been completed around the houses we returned to our homes, and, after my husband had marched for Delhi, a young lady—Miss Custance, daughter of Colonel Custance of the *carabiniers*—left the Dum-Dum to stay with me.

Though the inactivity of the *sepoys* added to our confidence and allowed of our emerging so far, still the country was considered most unsafe beyond our lines for any except armed parties.

The massacre of the garrison that surrendered at Cawnpore, of which we had garbled and unreliable accounts, had capped the folly and bloodthirstiness of the rebellion, had nerved every garrison with despair and every Field Force with revenge, and had thus done more to defeat the object of the rebels than any other act of the sad drama. England owes more to the massacre at Cawnpore than, perhaps, she will readily believe. We knew that between us and this revolt there could be no terms, no quarter, no rest; and when we looked on the gigantic task before us, utterly to destroy the army we had made, it was no wonder that many despaired of the result. Myriads in India listened with eager anxiety for intelligence from Delhi. Already tribes of natives away on the horizon of our Empire were gathering their arms, and songs of exultation were beginning to arise from those who hated our rule.

Even close to our cantonment a great brigade had passed, destroying the station of Haupper, almost within sight; and marching in triumph to Delhi, with miles of hackeries containing the plunder of Rohilcund.

The sullen sound of the Delhi artillery seldom failed to reach a listening ear in Meerut. In the stillness of the night its low roar now came with a deeper meaning, and caused a greater emotion than before. The roar of an enemy's gun sounds strangely, and carries with it as great a thrill to the heart of a soldier who hears it for the first time as to that of the citizen engaged in his peaceful pursuits.

But the siege was now hastening to its close. The great crisis had come; all the available force had been poured into the camp before the city, and it remained for General Wilson to take Delhi or to lose India.

Those who know India can alone fully comprehend the situation. All through the crisis our sway was greatly upheld by the force of opinion. The effects of a long career of victory cannot be effaced in an hour. There is reason to believe the opposition would have been more general if both princes and people had then not had an innate feeling of terror at exciting the wrath of the lordly lion, though half persuaded he was mortally wounded and his days numbered. To maintain this feeling an uninterrupted course of victory is necessary, or a blow so crushing that the previous check only makes its effects more visible.

Thus, Aliwal and Sobraon were required to restore the drawn battles of Moodkee and Ferozeshah, which shook our power to its foundation. It is therefore incumbent on us to overcome all opposition, for if a native ruler can erect a stronghold and successfully defy us, the country would quickly become covered with such fortifications and our rule with contempt. A check in the field, a delay in the storm of a city, excites far and near the attention of hostile communities, and may raise a commotion that would require a combined effort of the nation to withstand.

During a period of such intense and widespread excitement, which fixed on the proceedings in India the rapt attention of all its people, and of every nation of Asia, it became absolutely essential to re-establish our prestige by a stroke that smote into the dust the city most calculated to draw interest and to awake enthusiasm, and which had withstood our authority for many months. So, the prestige that told against the revolt in one way, told against ourselves in another; for while it frightened many a prince into good behaviour, it made the capture of Delhi and the advance of Havelock necessities of our existence, though both extremities of war.

It was under such trying circumstances that the *Maharajah* of Patiala, a neighbouring native prince, extended his aid to the Delhi Field Force, and evinced high moral courage and the greatest loyalty to the British Empire; keeping our communications open with the Punjaub, whence alone aid could come, and rendered possible the conveyance of the siege guns sent by Lord Lawrence, without which the storming of Delhi could not have been accomplished. This friendly prince is no longer alive, but when his son arrived in London to attend the Coronation, I wrote a short letter to a London paper expressing the hope that for the valuable help rendered to us in our critical position before Delhi, every consideration would be shown to his son during his visit to London, but no notice was taken of my letter, which, I suppose, found its way to the waste-paper basket.

On September 7th the operations commenced that were to decide the momentous question; and on the 20th the British ensign floated over the Imperial Palace. Short as was this interval, it was an age to me.

The country between Delhi and Meerut is almost as level as the floor of a room. By putting my ear to the ground, I could hear the guns, and by dint of practice I could detect any difference in sound. I at once perceived the opening of the siege guns and flew into the house to tell Miss Custance that the assault had begun. I looked at the clock and afterwards found I had been correct.

Although within sound of the guns our intelligence was often inaccurate and unreliable. The mails carried round by Paneeput took days to reach us; but on the morning following that great day, (September 14th, 1857), when the columns advanced to the storm of Delhi, a native runner arrived with the news. He said he had been borne across the bridge of boats in a throng so great that his feet could scarcely touch the ground, and the country around was covered with the fugitive army and denizens of the imperial city.

As rumours to this effect had often been received, the man was secured, with the promise of reward if the account proved true, and if false of a punishment which would have left him nothing more to hope for in this world. On receipt of further news our joy was considerably modified. An entrance had, indeed, been effected, though with immense loss of life, and the force was still fighting for its existence in the streets of Delhi.

The deep, low sound which had spoken such volumes to my heart had, indeed, ceased; yet I knew the warfare then going on to be more deadly, though less loud, and my anxiety was rather increased than diminished.

The country was hushed—every ear was open, every head outstretched for intelligence of this decisive struggle. Perhaps never before on so few British bayonets had hung so great a cause, and never before was news received in India by our race with more deep-felt joy and thankfulness to our Heavenly Preserver than that of the final and glorious close of this great siege.

Delhi was the lists where was fought out the challenge from the Native Army. The prize for the victor was India—for the vanquished, death.

When Delhi fell, the failure of the Mutiny was decided; and the after-campaign was a mere race of the vanquished from a pursuing fate.

It was not, however, the triumph to our arms, the display of British courage, nor the political results obtained that so filled with thankfulness the English community in these provinces; our lives were wrapped up in the siege; the existence of every Christian depended on the success of our force; and though England might have reconquered her Indian Empire had the attack failed, that Empire, till such reconquest, would undoubtedly have been lost.

CHAPTER 4.

I am not sure of the exact numbers, but, approximately, it has been computed that the loss on September 14th, the day of the assault on Delhi, was—

EUROPEANS.			NATIVES.		
	Killed.	Wounded.	Killed.		Wounded.
Officers . .	8 .	52	103	. . .	310
Rank and File	162 .	510			

Of course, as the street-fighting was kept up for a week, till we obtained possession of the palace on September 20th, the casualty list must have been much increased.

The entire effective force before Delhi has been estimated at:—

European Artillery	.	.	.	580	
,, Cavalry	.	.	.	514	
,, Infantry	.	.	.	2,672	
					3,766
Native Artillery	.	.	.	770	
,, Cavalry	.	.	.	1,313	
,, Infantry	.	.	.	3,417	
Engineers, Sappers, and Miners, etc.				722	
					6,222
		Grand Total	.	.	9,988

To the above add Cashmere contingent of 2,200 men with four guns, and cavalry of the Jhind *Rajah* 400 men, making the full number amount to 12,588.

The enemy at this time was believed to number 40,000 men.

It is not my intention to discuss the circumstances of the first, second, and third columns of attack on the city, but to confine myself to what occurred to the fourth column operating at Kissengunje, on which alone any controversy arose. This might have been thought impossible, as Colonel Muter did all that was done; he it was who sent in his despatch with those of the three others through Sir Archdale Wilson; he received commendation for the "judicious" way he withdrew the column out of the utmost confusion. He also was awarded his Brevet-Majority and the Command of the Hill Station of Murree, in the Punjaub, for this very service. Colonel Muter himself fretted over the position, because it had been impossible to advance. Subsequent operations proved that had the column penetrated into the city at that suburb, the whole of the little force would have been annihilated; for special care had been taken to render the entire distance to the Lahore Gate, as the *sepoys* thought, impregnable.

Sir John Kaye, in his dispassionate *History of the Sepoy War*, publishes the explanation Colonel Muter sent him, as he says, "detailing his own movements, and the events of which he was an eye-witness":—

My company (60th Rifles) led; subdivision advanced in skirmishing order; the other in support, at head of column. The movement, delayed for guns, which did not come, was then so rapid that the skirmishers could do little to cover. A bridge had to be crossed over a canal (dry) right under the walls of Kissengunje, held by the enemy in great strength, and the fire was heavy. Here Major Reid was wounded and his fall checked the advance of his Goorkhas he was leading. The 1st Bengal Fusiliers passed through at 'the double,' and continued the rush in front or along the wall, suffering from the fire as they made for the street which opened to the left and where the *sepoys* were gathered in force. Here, in front of the fusiliers, McBarnett was killed; as a captain, senior to me.

Then the 61st came up, but the confusion had become great as detachment after detachment got mingled on the other side of the bridge, with the enemy all the time firing from loopholes some fifty yards away. Parallel with the canal ran a low stone wall, behind which the exposed men sought shelter, and presently that wall was lined, and the fire against Kissengunje maintained. My men had joined in the rush of the detachments as they came up, and had got mixed in the *mêlée*, which made the position so peculiarly difficult for the various officers in command. We could neither give orders nor get them executed, and we were fighting with this deep canal (for it was deep and difficult) in our rear.

The Guides under Shebbeare had come up, and, having escaped the confusion into which the detachment had fallen on the failure of the dashes made in succession to gain the street, were comparatively in order. Shebbeare said, 'You had better assume the command. We must make a desperate effort to break away from this cover.' The 'assembly' was sounded, and soon a group of officers was gathered. Then the 'advance' and, waving our swords, we went over the wall calling on the men to follow. The bugle notes aroused the enemy, and the fire became furious—so withering that it was almost impossible to live for a few minutes exposed to it.

The adjutant of the Guides was killed as he mounted the wall. Shebbeare was shot through the cheek, and the number who fell on the instant effectually checked the movement. Having failed in this I went to our right to see if we could work round, and there I met the engineer officer, with whom I consulted. To take ground to our right would be to expose our position on the range to attack, utterly denuded of troops, all being drawn off for the attack on Delhi. While speaking to the Engineer officer he was, as we all supposed, mortally wounded. Then I returned to see how we could best withdraw, and heard that Shebbeare had been again hit. It was under these circumstances I decided to send a message to the Crow's Nest Battery to open on the enemy regardless of us.

A young officer carried that message with great rapidity, and while awaiting the opening of the big guns I encouraged the withdrawal of the wounded, and by this time, for we had been long under fire, the force had considerably dwindled. Lieutenant Evans, the young artillery officer in charge of the Crow's Nest Battery, had fortunately prepared for the emergency, and he could see from his commanding height that our attack had failed. With the utmost precision, he pitched his shrapnel over our heads and enabled us to withdraw with an ease otherwise impossible. But for this, the retreat might have been disastrous. I have always given Lieutenant Evans great credit for his part in this, both for being prepared and for the way in which the guns were handled in a fire of shrapnel directed a few feet over our heads. The representation I made procured for Shebbeare the Victoria Cross, which he had well earned.

When Major Reid got well, he took me over the ground to show what he intended. His design was to run close up to the wall and along it, trusting to the enemy being unable to shoot straight down—almost perpendicularly—on to the street, up which, if he could sweep, he hoped to get the *sepoys* on the run and keep them going. But he fell, and no one on the field knew his plan.

When we were at Murree, where my husband was commanding the station, given the appointment for this very service, Major Richard Lawrence was there, and General Sir Henry Norman wrote a series of questions relating to the fourth column attack on Kissengunje. Colonel Muter immediately wrote for an interview with Major Lawrence to talk the matter over and compare notes; but Major Lawrence declined. Colonel Muter wanted to be perfectly accurate. At Delhi there was no question about the facts. Major Lawrence had no troops at Kissengunje, for the Cashmeries made their attack in another column.

When some years ago I published my experiences in the Mutiny and elsewhere, I wished to introduce my husband's part in the fourth column, but he prevented me, saying I was writing my recollections, not his, and the mistake has been, that, in common with all brave men, he has been too modest. Major Lawrence, who came in a political, not a military capacity, contended that he should have succeeded to the command of the column on the fall of Major Reid, but as he did not, and in the exigencies of the struggle my husband did all that was possible, it seems childish to raise such a question.

Major Lawrence objected to three passages in the narrative of the *Siege of Delhi*, published by Sir Henry Norman:—

1. The fourth column, under Major Reid, advanced from the Subzee Mundi towards Kissengunje, the *Cashmere contingent* co-operating on its right. The latter, however, was so sharply attacked by the insurgents who were in great force, that, after losing a great number of men and four guns, *they were completely defeated and fell back to camp.*

2. Major Reid's column met with the most strenuous opposition, *greatly increased doubtless by the failure of the Cashmere contingent.*

3. Captain Muter, 60th Rifles, the *next senior officer, judiciously withdrew the troops to their former posts* at Hindoo Raos and in the Subzee Mundi.

(N.B. The italics are not mine).

It is well known that without guns the little force would simply have been annihilated had it persevered in the attack.

DESPATCH OF CAPTAIN DUNBAR DOUGLAS MUTER, 1ST BATT. 60TH ROYAL RIFLES, ON FOURTH COLUMN OF ATTACK AT SIEGE OF DELHI.

From Captain D. D. Muter, Her Majesty's 1st Battalion 60th Royal Rifles, to Major R. S. Ewart, Deputy-Assistant Adjutant-General, dated Camp, Delhi, September 17th, 1857.

At dawn on September 14th the column of attack on Kishengunje, in the order and strength as shown in the list following, was drawn up at the Subsee Mundee Serai, under the command of Major Reid.

The Jummo contingent commenced the attack before our artillery had arrived, and Major Reid, wishing to support the attack, moved down the road in a column of fours, covered by twenty-five Riflemen in skirmishing order.

The enemy opened fire from the bridge over the canal, and from

60 Rifles	50
Sirmoor Battalion . .	200
1st Fusiliers	160
Guides Infantry . .	200
Coke's Corps . . .	25
Kumaon Battalion . .	65
Her Majesty's 61st Regiment	80
Total men . .	780

behind walls and the loop-holed *serai* of Kishengunje. Major Reid fell wounded in the head. The fall of their gallant leader checked the advance of the Gurkhas. The fusiliers came to the front at the double, led by Captain Wriford.

The rush of the Rifles and fusiliers placed them for a moment in possession of the breastwork at the end of the *serai*, but those men, unsupported, were unable to maintain the position under the heavy flanking fire to which they were exposed.

The native troops lined a garden to the right of the road, and Lieutenant R. H. Shebbeare, whose gallantry in this trying affair was the admiration of every one, with a few of the Guides and some Europeans, took possession of a mosque. Every effort was made here to reform the troops, and charge the enemy's position, but without success, though many officers sacrificed themselves in the attempt.

As I observed columns of the enemy's horse and foot taking ground to our right, and as I saw they were in great force to our front and left flank, I considered the object of the attack so far gained in having directed the attention of the enemy from the main point of attack. Fearing also that the enemy's great strength might encourage him to attack our batteries on the hill, I thought it right, as I had succeeded to the command on the fall of Major Reid, to re-occupy the position from which we had been withdrawn. This was accomplished with little further loss, under cover of the Crow's Nest Battery, which fired shrapnel and shell a few feet over our heads, and with the most admirable precision and fatal effect to the enemy.

This battery was commanded by Lieutenant H. J. Evans, of the artillery.

I cannot close this report without mentioning the noble way in which two officers and one sergeant fell in the attack. Captain G. G. McBarnet, attached to the 1st Bengal Fusiliers, died at the head of his men at the first rush, and Lieutenant A. W. Murray, of the Guides, was killed while gallantly seconding his immediate superior, Lieutenant Shebbeare, who was himself struck by two bullets. I am much disappointed in learning that Sergeant Dunleary, of the fusiliers, a man whose conduct was conspicuous throughout, was killed in the field.

Annexed is a statement of our loss, which, I regret to say, has been very heavy.

★★★★★★

The street-fighting, after an entry had been effected, was of a trying and dangerous character, The *khansamah* afterwards told me that on one occasion when he had got into a house in a street the 60th were occupying, he spread a serviette for a table-cloth, and had got a good steak for the *Sahib's* dinner, but the *sepoys* regained possession of the street and the dinner was lost—procured with such difficulty. The officers poured out the wines and spirits into the streets lest they should demoralize the men. The *sepoys* hoped our troops would become intoxicated and useless to us.

An obelisk to the memory of those of the 1st Battalion 60th Royal Rifles, officers and men, who fell at Delhi has been erected at Dover.

CHAPTER 5

As giving several graphic details of what occurred at Meerut at the time of the outbreak, yet never hinting at the great service my husband performed in saving the Treasury, which he simply regarded in the light of ordinary duty, I think this article will interest the reader:—

INCIDENTS OF THE *SEPOY* MUTINY
(From *Englishman*, Calcutta.)
By Colonel D. D. Muter.

On New Year's Day (1858) the *Daily Telegraph* published one of those life-like sketches of sporting men which often emanated from the pen of the Hon. Francis Lawley. On the subject of "Turf Reminiscences" that writer had no equal; and although I know nothing of racing and only met General Anson when Commander-in-Chief in India, his graphic account brought vividly to my memory a picture that had almost faded from my recollection. The story moves around Newmarket and high life in London; but its sequel is in India in the most stormy and threatening period of British rule.

The grace with which Mr. Lawley introduces Mrs. Anson is one of the charms of his style, and it recalls the scene shortly before the

MONUMENT ERECTED ON "THE RIDGE" BEFORE DELHI
TO THE MEMORY OF THOSE WHO FELL IN THE SIEGE

MEMORIAL ERECTED AT DOVER TO OFFICERS AND MEN OF THE
'DELHI FIELD FORCE" WHO DIED IN THE OPERATIONS, 1857

Mutiny, when the party on their way from Calcutta to Simla halted at Meerut, the great cantonment formed to overawe the fortified city of Delhi, distant, as the crow flies, thirty miles, our strongest arsenal, the seat of dynasty which still titularly maintained the insignia of royalty, and was regarded with veneration amounting to superstition everywhere among Mahometans.

The Mutiny was there being planned, and the intention was for the native troops to surround the British force, unarmed in church, and precipitate the revolt by a massacre that would startle the world. General and Mrs. Anson attended divine service, and, if I do not mistake, the Bishop of Madras on that Sunday preached on the text, "*There shall be showers of blessings.*" The bishop had, perhaps, scarcely got back to his own diocese before these showers fell in brimstone and fire on the land he had left, as over Sodom and Gomorrah.

The party of the commander-in-chief was grouped outside; the ladies waiting for their carriage to draw up, and the Colonel of 1st Battalion 60th Royal Rifles—a battalion to which the country owes a debt of gratitude—descended the steps. I saw the ladies turn their heads to conceal a smile as the gallant officer hobbled down, for though a fine man, he was infirm on his feet. He lived to command an army, to obtain the *sobriquet* of "The Avenger" and to die a distinguished general, yet he did not present the *beau ideal* of a Rifleman. The Ansons passed up to Simla and, shortly after, Mrs. Anson—said in her day to have been one of the most beautiful women in London—and her daughter returned to the more congenial if less bright clime of their native land. Neither she nor her husband were destined again to meet; and both were reserved for tragic deaths.

The mutineers did not succeed in carrying out their plan of surprising and massacring the British in the church; but the native regiments rose on Sunday, May 10th, 1857, and the tumult, and sound of musketry and roar of voices filled the air as the soldiers gathered unarmed on the parade ground for divine service that afternoon.

Presently the whole camp was alive, and the profound stillness of the European portion of the large cantonment was stirred as by inspiration. From every direction the native guards were stealing away, and soon wounded men and others who had fled for their lives hurried into the barracks to tell their tale of murder and rapine. Without any word of command, all the soldiers in their white clothing rushed towards their lines, and quick as thought came streaming out dressed in green and accoutred. Before the officers had assembled the parade had been changed from peace to war, and shortly after the solid heavy tread of troops on the march was heard along the roads leading to the parade grounds that faced the *sepoy* quarter.

As the British force drew up in front of the native lines, extending perhaps a mile and a half, the whole was a wall of flame, a conflagration few men had ever witnessed in extent. It fell to the writer to direct the first fire opened in the Mutiny. Sir Archdale Wilson, the Brigadier, had ridden away under the bullets of his own guard, and my company, as the advance guard of the force, had been thrown into skirmishing order when the troops defiled on the "*maidan*."

Sir Archdale was close behind and I went to him and asked:—"Are we to load with bullets and shoot straight?"

"Yes; for execution, you see the position;"—and the men loaded. As they drew near the babel of voices rising from behind the sheet of flame directed the first bullets, which I may add were from Enfield rifles, then a novelty in the army, and only just introduced at Meerut; indeed, to its cartridge the Mutiny has been with some truth ascribed. As our bullets tore through the gardens around the officers' houses, cutting down bushes and singing in the ears of the *Pandies*, the hubbub drew away towards the road to Delhi, hastened by the horse artillery, which, galloping up and unlimbering, made it hotter for those behind the wall of flame.

What followed is a matter of history. Delhi fell to the mutineers; the emperor was recognised as their sovereign; and the British in their cantonment were face to face with the *Sepoy* Army gathering in force in the Imperial city, fortified, having inside its walls the chief arsenal of the country, with all the siege artillery and munitions of war in their possession.

The fight for the Empire that followed has not yet been fully told. On it hinged at least the immediate fate of India and the lives of nearly all the Europeans. Nothing but a series of providences saved the position, which looked as black as night when the commander-in-chief descended from the hills and reached as far as Kurnaul on May 27th, just seventeen days after the outbreak. That cantonment, long ago the great frontier camp, was an abandoned station not far from Delhi, a scene of desolation with houses once handsome, tenanted only by wild animals, and falling into ruin, presenting a type, when the general reached his last resting-place, of what India would be from the Sutlej to the sea if he failed in his mission.

The general had descended from the serene and genial temperature of Simla, at an elevation of 7,000 feet, into the plains, to move in tents through an atmosphere which danced and glowed, for you can there see the heat in May. The wind passed as through a furnace. Nothing living appeared on the white baked plain after the sun had well risen. A fruitful land bore the appearance of an arid desert, but terrible as was the contrast in climate, politically and martially the position was infinitely more trying. No man knew what the day might bring forth. If the Punjaub rose, India was lost. If the Gwalior contingent, the best appointed and finest of the feudatory forces, marched on Delhi as a hostile army, the British force must be swallowed up. Fortunately, the native princes waited in a similar uncertainty on events, to learn how they would turn before anything decisive had happened. General Anson succumbed under the terrible trial and died of cholera at Kurnaul.

Mr. Lawley says that when General Anson was gazetted to the command in India the newspapers with one accord, always hard and unjust to racing and sporting men who endeavour to be something else, "opened fire on the obscure and untried soldier." Yet General Anson died in harness, weighed down by the tremendous exertion required to set that army in motion, he himself taking the lead. Such was the nature of the work thus suddenly thrown upon the chief, that the general who succeeded on his death, hardly lasted three months, and was buried near the city before which the small British Force Anson gathered, toiled and died; and perhaps no regiment ever more greatly distinguished itself than did that 1st Battalion 60th Rifles, though there were no war correspondents on the spot to send home the accounts which gave the place of honour to Lucknow as if the vital struggle had not centred at Delhi.

Sir Archdale Wilson, who had succeeded on the death in succession of the two senior officers, had to endure—perhaps with all the more persistency because his communication was only open in one direction—the same "on to Richmond" cry which broke many a Union general during the great Confederate War. Lord Lawrence was peremptory in his demand that Delhi should be taken or the army would perish. Better lose the army than the Empire; and if action is not prompt, the Empire will be lost. When at last Sir Archdale broke into the city and pushed his columns through its thoroughfares in the vain effort to sweep out its hordes, he was foiled all round. He held one corner, and had it not been for a gallant engineer officer he might have fallen back.

On September 14th the assault was delivered, and for a whole

STORMING OF DELHI

week the fight in the city was maintained. All the time the Gwalior contingent, the most complete Native Army in India, hung like a storm-cloud over the operations, but native like, it moved, after Delhi had fallen and India had been saved, to meet the advancing regiments fresh from England, and inflicted on Wyndham's a defeat at Cawnpore.

The "showers of blessings," which do not come as we regard blessings, are realised long after the events that startle and confound us. General Anson perished among the first victims, perhaps almost in despair of saving the country. Strange to say, there was a native prophecy that one hundred years after Plassy, the *Raj* of "John Company" would end. This proved to be true; but did not fit into the conclusion of the mutineers. The East India Commercial Company ceased, and the rule passed to the queen. The restrictions beyond which that Empire had grown were removed, and a more enlightened sway followed on the overthrow brought by the great Mutiny.

In the sketch an incidental remark tells how isolated, cut off from all communication was the force collected by Anson at Umballa and by Sir Archdale Wilson at Meerut, for though the commander-in-chief died May 27th, it was not till the middle of July that the fact appears to have reached England. We were literally in the midst of a population apparently, but not really hostile, the army only knowing and commanding within the limits its scouts could reach. By observation from the heights overlooking Delhi held by our outposts, the arrivals of fresh garrisons of mutineers only became known by the stir in the city and the sure attack which next day followed; the fight for life often being inside these lines perpetrated by men wearing British uniforms, acting under British words of command, and using arms from British arsenals.

This awful trial of endurance lasted for months, but may be said to have culminated on the hundredth anniversary of the Battle of Plassy, when the most protracted and determined attack was defeated. Never after did the *sepoy* fight as before—it was then the struggle for life—not for Empire.

GENERAL JOHN NICHOLSON
(Who commanded the storming party in the assault on Delhi. He was
shot through the chest and died a few days later)

Part 2: Delhi

CHAPTER 6

The fall of Delhi opened a direct communication between Meerut and the Field Force, and several officers took the opportunity to pass to and from the capital city. My husband sent to me to say it was safe for me to come to Delhi and to lay my *dak* (posting carriage) at the time Sir John Jones was to go. I did so, and about 3 a.m. was awaiting the *gharry* (carriage) in some trepidation, as I had not yet left the queen's lines since the first night of the outbreak, when suddenly I heard the *purdah* (curtain) pulled aside, and in came my husband, bronzed beyond recognition, wearing a beard that covered his chest, but on his face the ever-welcome smile of affection and pleasure. For fully five minutes I lost all power of speech, the surprise was so great.

"Come," he said, "we must not delay. I felt so uneasy at the thought you would travel alone, as there are still native cavalry roaming about, that I applied for twenty-four hours' leave in order to fetch you, so we will go together in your *dak gharree* now at our door."

Only those who had gone through my ordeal of anxiety and apprehension can realise the delight of that journey to Delhi, which we reached at sunrise. By some means best known to themselves, our allies, the good little Goorkhas, had obtained a hint of our proceedings, and as we approached the gate all those in the neighbourhood turned out and gave us a rousing cheer. The Goorkhas always fraternised with the 60th, who they termed their *bhais* or brothers.

I found I was the first lady to enter the city after it had come into our hands. I arrived on October 17th, after having been immured in our lines at Meerut since May 10th.

The battalion was quartered in the palace, a word that will give a false idea to those who do not know the East, and it was decided that we should there remain for the ensuing winter.

Assault of Delhi: Capture of the Cashmere Gate

The late residence of the Timour family is enclosed within a wall three miles in extent, enormous in height, with bastions and fortified gates, embrasures and rows of loopholes. It is faced with slabs of red sandstone as if built of blocks, giving it a grand and massive appearance.

Within this wall are the houses of the emperor, mosques, halls of justice and of audience, gardens with numerous summer-houses, and the courtyards pertaining to His Majesty. Yet these form only a part of the whole, as there are barracks for the three regiments the king was allowed to keep, and dwellings for retainers of all degrees, from the establishments of princes of the blood to the huts of the coolies, making up a population of 10,000 persons. The rule of the *Mogul* had narrowed till this circle represented his dominions; but here he had reigned supreme, with the power, I believe, of life and death.

The principal gate, in grand proportions equalling any other in the world, faced the principal street of Delhi, called the Chandnee Chowk, or Silver Street, occupied by a large proportion of the jewellers of whom Delhi is justly proud.

When I entered, one of its massive portals hung a tottering ruin on a hinge, blown in by Colonel Sir John Jones when his column advanced to the capture, just four weeks before. The mouths of three great guns were pointed to the entrance, as when placed by the enemy for the reception of this column. A fine arcade, gaily painted, and lined on each side with shops, leads to an open square. The doors of the stalls were riddled with bullets, and instead of the *buniahs* (shopkeepers) with their goods, they were filled with the flat, ugly faces of the little Goorkhas.

Two years before I had entered this arcade; then it was occupied by a crowd of the king's guard, and I was forbidden to proceed without the written order of Captain Douglas, who lived over the gate where the family in this fearful rebellion had been savagely murdered.

In the centre of the square the road goes by a tank, and in this was perpetrated one of the massacres that it will take years to forgive. The women and children who escaped death on May 11th and 12th were after many days' confinement butchered there in cold blood; and this deed was sanctioned by the king in his own territory.

A paved road leads through an archway to a great gate on the right, facing another fine street, and on the left passes on to the Fort of Selimghur, lined by the dry bed of a canal which formerly supplied this fatal tank with water. The court was filled with guns, waggons, and army materials of all sorts, showing by dents and broken wheels marks of severe service. I saw the uniform of the Rifles on guard in a building we passed under, and then we entered a fine court, and faced a grand edifice called the *Amm-Kass*, or Hall of Justice, occupied by what the siege had left of the battalion. The way to the private courts of the king was through an arch on one side of the *Amm-Kass*, but we were driven to the other side where I could see no exit. On the top of the Justice Hall I noticed a strange structure, but it appeared stranger still when I was told it was my new abode.

I was wondering how this position could be reached when the *gharry* stopped, and I was led, by a passage broken through a house behind the *Amm-Kass*, to a flight of steps up to the top of a wall broad enough for a carriage drive. This singular road, elevated more than twenty feet, wound through the palace to houses, and around court-yards. A few paces to the left, another range of large stone steps led under the quaint structure to a handsome court with a marble fountain in the centre, carved elaborately, and inlaid with carnelian, bloodstone and agate. The golden letters of the inscription had been abstracted, some of the stones had been picked out, and the fountain was dry, as were all in this palace, which had once sparkled so brilliantly with flowing and with jetting water.

But the house most interested me, and I confess to a chill of despair when I turned to examine it. What had formerly been for the king a pretty summer residence, was now to me a cold wintry ruin, without windows, without doors, without even a floor. A shell had torn up the pavement, and the huge rent in the walls, considering the perilous elevation, aroused an unpleasant feeling of insecurity. A closer inspection, and a little time for thought, enabled me to see how the place could be made habitable. Below, two rooms were large and lofty, and smaller ones branched from them; above, a quaint one-room construction stood on the roof, with its little courtyard facing the river, while that below looked towards the city. Thus, house rose on house to a pinnacle, the architect having apparently played with brick and mortar as children play with cards.

For some time, I was superintending masons, painters, and carpenters, and restoring what appeared to be a century of neglect.

But the whole palace of the *Moguls* was a sad picture of dilapidation and dirt. Dirt overlaid everything, dimmed the brightness of paint, and sullied the purity of marble. Mud walls, erected without an apparent object, hid the choicest specimens of architectural beauty, and coats of whitewash covered blocks of sculptured stone. The first appearance raised a doubt if it were indeed the dwelling of Akbar, the residence of Shah Jehan. A more correct knowledge of this celebrated seat of government showed that debased descendants filled the place of refined ancestors. On the *Dewan-Kass*, or "Hall of Audience," are inscribed in gold the lines that now form so singular a contrast to the fact, and are thus translated by Moore in *Lalla Rookh*:—

If there is a Paradise on earth,
It is this, it is this.

From my house, if it still stands, the view is grand in extent, in beauty, and in interest. The palace, the city, the country lay as a map at our feet; and in every direction we looked through a clear atmosphere on a panorama I believe to be unequalled in India.

The giant walls of the palace rose in a battlemented circle around, and from this high post in its centre we gazed on its gardens, its squares, its streets, and all its varied buildings. The grey old Fort of Selimghur frowned on the Jumna, which, coursing close to the city wall, there divided, and sent a rapid and romantic-looking stream between the dark turrets of the ancient fort and the gay red walls of the palace. The water was spanned by two bridges—one hoary as Selimghur, the other light and elegant as the palace—a singular contrast between grey age and gay youth.

Far as I could see, the Jumna came winding down through the rich and level country, running close by, and away into the distance, where its glancing waters borrowed the azure of the sky, and the muddy current became in hue as ultramarine.

The palace hung over the water; its battlemented wall ceased where it reached the scarped bank which wound with the channel, rising from the water some twenty feet and faced with blocks of stone. The ground within the palace was level with the top, and it was on the crest of this scarp that the Moslem architect had lavished all his skill, and the result in its day must have been one of rare and tasteful beauty.

Buildings were massed together and piled on each other with quaint projections and curiously carved windows jutting over the water, and among them, conspicuous in beauty, stood out the *Dewan-Kass*.

A seat of solid crystal like a block of massive ice was placed in a window, which from its delicate tracery seemed spun from marble—a fit spot for such a seat and not unworthy of him who styled himself "Ruler of the World."

Next to this, the waters of the river reflected the trees of a garden, and among them were domes and minarets, mosques and summer-houses, difficult to describe—all of them small, but of exquisite material and finish. It was from the island where stands Selimghur that the scene broke with so singular a beauty on the sight; from my elevation the plan was clear, but the details were lost.

What strikes a stranger most forcibly is the way in which the Moslem artist had revelled in water. From a marble summer-house that looked along the crest of the scarp, a stream had flowed in a little cataract down an inlaid slab of this stone, still resting on its old incline, and, passing under the floor had been conducted in a marble canal into a series of buildings adjoining the *Dewan-Kass*, where it had filled marble fountains and had circled into marble baths. The canal was dry and almost choked with rubbish, and the visitor now entered rooms whose singular construction amazed him, and could only be accounted for by the fact that they had been erected to receive the falling showers of fountains.

A large square tank stood in the centre of the garden, and from the middle rose a curious structure of red stone, connected with the bank by a bridge that now passed over its dry bed, on which a boat lay rotting. Straight-paved walls and straight lines of trees gave a formal aspect to the grounds quite out of character with the style of the houses. Still, from above, the deep foliage hid these defects. The whole presented a scene more of neglect, almost amounting to barbarism, than of ruin, and with the water was gone the life and glory of the place.

Beyond the decaying seat of these degenerate kings, I looked over a city more beautiful far, when thus seen, than any other I had yet beheld. Its small size being enclosed within walls about seven miles in extent, placed it all before me. I could almost trace the line of fortifications, with its gates and bastions, in its entire circuit. The wide streets, the principal houses, not hidden in masses of green foliage, the mosques and the temples, marked distinctly the districts in which they were situated.

Straight before me the Chandnee Chowk, with its lines of trees, ran grandly up to the Lahore Gate, cutting the city in halves. To the left was a dense region of houses, where, from a slight elevation conspicuous in its huge proportions, rose the *Jumma Musjid*, its dome towering over all roofs, and its two minarets raising their elegant spires far above the dome. In all directions from this great Moslem temple the streets branched away like a spider's web.

The region on the right had been evidently the fashionable quar-

Chandni Chowk, or Silver Street: The Jewellers' Quarter in Delhi

ter, and its great houses peeped here and there from behind the leaves of numberless trees. I looked into the arsenal, over the wall so gallantly defended on May 11th, on the rows of cannon and piles of shot that remained, but the college beyond was concealed by the brandling boughs. The church alone of all the buildings clearly showed its dome and held up above them its golden cross.

Far over the city the Flagstaff Tower, the Observatory and Hindoo Rao's—names so familiar to all in India—standing on the brow of a rocky height, were sharply defined against the blue sky.

That height is now enshrined in history. Between it and this spot the great fight had been fought, every position had been contested, and every yard was over a grave. The whole way was strewn with the wreck left by the war—a wreck not visible from where I stood, for the scene, which had been beautifully laid out, looked as lovely now as it had done before that fatal May. The leaves were as green, the white road passed round the tower as if uninjured by a shell, and the ruin of Hindoo Rao's only added to the picturesque effect.

I did not know, as I gazed, that scarcely a human being was left in the silent city at my feet. All I yet knew of war was confined to the losses of our own people by battle and exposure, and I was ignorant of the awful destruction that had overtaken the inhabitants. It had not occurred to me that there were sufferers greater than ourselves with whom I ought to sympathize.

In the building beneath me, where the Mogul emperors had administered justice, were lodged the third, left after the perils of the siege, of that noble battalion which had marched on May 25th from Meerut. The room, supported on a forest of pillars, was gigantic in size. The emperor ascended from a private staircase at the back, and entering a raised dais of beautiful marble exquisitely carved, seated himself on that great throne which became the prey of Nadir Shah, and whose noblest gem now sparkles among the jewels of our queen. This was the celebrated Peacock Throne, and that diamond the Koh-i-noor.

Here it was the emperors held their public *durbars*, met ambassadors and administered justice; but the private audience was in the *Dewan-Kass*, rising, as I have said, from the scarped bank of the river, and looking down on the Jumna. In that hall the last emperor was tried by a commission of British officers, where not many years before he had considered himself disgraced and a stain cast on his escutcheon, because a governor-general, and one of England's highest nobles, had sat down in his presence.

Lahore Gate, Delhi

Shortly after my arrival I drove over the field of the recent struggles. The advanced batteries had not yet been removed, though coolies were beginning the work. The country was pretty between the walls and the hills, circling together for more than a mile, and maintaining an average breadth of about the same distance, the space between tastefully laid out and intersected by roads which here and there were rough with the boulders that had rolled from the rocky height and overgrown with a tangled vegetation. The air was fresh and exhilarating and all looked bright on this autumn morning. The road passed close by the round Flagstaff Tower which I had looked on with interest from my elevated residence. The women and children assembled there when the mutineers from Meerut and the Delhi brigade joined them in open rebellion.

Behind the circling hill was the ruined cantonment, and the long lines could still be traced where the tents of the British force had stood. A good road runs along the crest of the hill, and, passing the Observatory, we drove by it to a ruin of great interest. This was the solid and handsome house of Hindoo Rao, a wealthy native gentleman, who had given his name to the principal post of the besieging army, and the scene of innumerable combats. The entire front had been battered to pieces, and it was owing to the solidity of the structure that any portion of it still stood.

The rooms so long occupied by the gallant little Goorkhas were pointed out to me, and a small apartment behind, where a shot from Kissengunje had burst, killing or dreadfully wounding nearly every man in the room. But Hindoo Rao's had been the scene of so many tragedies, the deathplace of so many brave soldiers, that this shot is only remarkable for the wholesale nature of the destruction it effected. The ground was torn up by the projectiles and shot, and pieces of shell lay thickly strewn around.

Looking down on the city the eye rested on the Morree Bastion, the destroyer of Hindoo Rao's, now itself a heap of ruins; and halfway between, as it appeared to me, a swarm of coolies were at work demolishing the battery that had smashed the bastion into an undistinguishable mass.

The long line of wall between the Lahore and the Cashmere gates seemed little injured, but as the wall neared the Cashmere Gate the effects of the fire were more apparent.

The singular beauty of Delhi was seen to even greater advantage from Hindoo Rao's than from the structure at the top of the *Amm*

Kass. It combined the grace of Moslem architecture with the charm of English finish. Through trees and bungalows wound smooth mac-adamised roads; beyond were the fortifications. Still farther away rose domes and minarets, and behind all were the dark red walls of the palace. From green trees peeped the roofs of houses, and these were broken by spires and *pagodas*; and I feel sure that, even during the worst period of peril and anxiety, many who looked from that height with the fierce determination utterly to destroy the city must have acknowledged in their hearts that its beauty was beyond that of any other they had seen.

The hill from Hindoo Rao's slopes down to the *Subsi-Mundi*, and I passed on the way two or three batteries, such as the "Crow's Nest," a name with which I was familiar. At the base of the hill ran the high road between Delhi and Umballa, and beyond was the suburb of Kissengunje, held by the enemy in great force during the siege, and where the fourth column had been compelled to retire after sustaining terrible loss.

The *Subsi-Mundi* is a large square *serai*, and was the point on the extreme right of the British position. The operations of the force were conducted between it and the River Jumna; but the enemy had a battery on the right enfilading the height, and a battery on the left throwing its shot across the river. Thus, the besiegers were themselves besieged, and the beleaguered city had by far a wider scope of communication than the beleaguering force.

On our return we passed the handsome house of Sir Theophilus Metcalfe, now a sad picture of wanton destruction. Between it and the Cashmere Gate this cruel war had everywhere left its mark; cannon-balls had splintered walls and cut trees to pieces; shells had dug holes in the road, and every log of timber was penetrated by a stray bullet. The houses were in ruins, but the ruin in the country was mere play when contrasted with that in the town.

The fortifications were shattered, the gates lay on the ground, the bridge across the moat bore heavy traces of the strife, and the neighbourhood showed how large a portion of the fire had been concentrated on the Cashmere Gate.

This gate was the scene of some striking incidents of the Mutiny. By it the troops advanced from the cantonment to meet the mutineers from Meerut. There the officers first became convinced how little the *sepoys* they had led were to be relied on; many escaped over the adjacent walls, and above it a British magistrate is said to have been

BLOWING-UP OF THE CASHMERE GATE AT DELHI

While endeavouring to fire the charge, Lieut. Salkeld was shot through the arm and leg, and handed over the slow match to Corporal Burgess, who fell mortally wounded just as he had accomplished the onerous duty hanged. There gallantly had died most of the party who had blown in the gate, and up that incline had rushed the assaulting column.

Where I stood had first rung the cheers of the British Army on the day the fate of India was placed in their hands. It is singular to relate that on this spot, not long after, a starving multitude of natives—when the country groaned under a famine—were fed by British hands from the proceeds of British charity; a noble sequel to the sad story, and one, I trust, that may be remembered to England's honour, if the acts of her sons during this dreadful period were not always tempered with justice and with mercy.

The first building of importance within the gates—the Protestant church—had not escaped a tremendous battering, though the chaplain declared that the cross that surmounted the dome was uninjured. The *Delhi Gazette* press, the college for native students, the house of Khan Mahommed Khan and of Colonel Skinner were either totally destroyed or much damaged, and the walls and the ground were pitted with the marks of bullets and of shell.

Farther on we passed the magazine Lieutenant Willoughby so gallantly attempted to destroy. Up a street to the right, bearing marks of the severe struggle, we entered a garden, with the remains of a splendid house standing in the centre. When the Mutiny began it was occupied by the Delhi Bank, and became the tomb of the manager and of all his family. The murderers had rioted there in plunder and in destruction, and on it Brigadier Campbell had fallen back, after his brilliant advance to the walls of the Jumma Musjid. It had been strongly fortified, and was still covered by sandbags, as it had been held during the period of the street fighting from September 14th to the occupation of the palace.

A short street led into the Chandnee Chowk, a more melancholy picture still, than any I had yet seen. When last I looked on this fine street, not many months before, it presented a gay and joyous sight; broad as it is, it was scarcely broad enough for the throng that filled it. Elephants and camels, horses and carriages, decked with the finery of the East, crowded the way; now it was silent and empty. The contents of the shops lay strewn in the street, or huddled in a confused mass on the floors. The sneaking figure of some prowling thief, a lean, half-famished dog, or one of the many cats—the sole inhabitants of Delhi—were all that moved. The painful effect of this solitude was more depressing than even the ruin. Where were the people of Delhi? The tender children, the delicate women, the old and infirm, all were gone, swept away by the fatal crimes of others!

Those who know war, not from books, but from experience of its realities, shrink from it with horror; and a war like this, without quarter and without mercy is the worst affliction that can overtake a land. No city desolated by a plague ever wore the appearance of Delhi at that time, or became the solitude it then was.

Before many months elapsed nearly every great city in the immense Central Provinces of India was stormed or occupied by our army; and the loss of life, the destruction of property, the cruel sufferings, will never be known to the world unless a second Macaulay wholly devotes himself to the task.

Right in the centre of the Chandnee Chowk a hideous erection of wood was the only new and uninjured structure—and this was the gallows. Hundreds perished on that platform, and among the number were *rajahs* and *nawabs* who had themselves and their fathers before them ruled in the territory around. I trust that no innocent men died there, victims to the fierce hatred the massacres had excited.

A war like this, however, acts with the fellest injustice, and were the number of blameless persons who were sacrificed truly estimated, the British public would be horrified at the result. When Colonel Muter was visiting the advanced posts on the capture of Bareilly he was asked by the officer in command what was to be done with some women who had been taken out of a well. The officer led him into a small enclosure where stretched on the ground lay the dead bodies of six or seven girls who evidently belonged to the upper classes.

Beside them were five or six others slowly recovering, and an old woman rocking herself on her knees and pouring out her sorrows in prayer. The officer pointed to a narrow well, down the black depths of which my husband looked, but he could see no bottom. These women had precipitated themselves into this hole, springing down one after another, amid the crash of shell and storm of shot preceding the advance of the troops to the capture of the city.

CHAPTER 7

When the workmen had finished, we were in possession of a good sitting-room, dining-room and bedroom, with a dressing-room at either end. The building was too much exposed for comfort in the season now approaching. It was not till the end of November that I really knew what the cold of a Delhi winter morning was. The wind howled through every crevice, and whirled the dust in eddies around the outer court. At night it whistled loudly around the corners of my singular house, and piles of blankets failed to keep me warm. In the day, I heaped up logs on the low-lying fire, and this threw out a strong heat. The climate during the winter is fine, dry, clear, cold, and invigorating. People unacquainted with India picture to themselves the country for the whole year under a tropical sun, but they have little idea either of the fierceness of the heat in summer, or of the cold of the blasts of winter in the North-west Provinces.

The supplies were abundant, and we experienced no difficulty from the commencement of the war in procuring all we required. English stores, of course, rose enormously; but everything grown in the country remained cheap and plentiful. A fowl could be purchased for a shilling, a dozen eggs one shilling and threepence, mutton and beef about sixpence per pound. Vegetables and fish were cheaper still; while hares, snipe, and wildfowl were abundant in the market. The Chandnee Chowk began to reassume some appearance of life, and while the rest of Delhi was a wilderness, shops and stalls were open there to supply the Force quartered in the city.

No English mail had yet reached us, though news came by indirect sources, and we were gratified to learn how deep was the interest excited throughout the civilised world by the ardent struggle of the English in India. England had hastened to our rescue—the sea was covered with steamers full of troops. Batteries of artillery and squadrons of cavalry were pouring in by the overland route, and Sir Colin Campbell had assumed the command-in-chief. From other parts came the intelligence of the advance of Havelock, the relief of Lucknow, and the victories of Sir Hugh Rose; and we looked hopefully for the time when this devastating war would cease.

The ignorance and folly of the men who had originated the Mutiny became more strikingly displayed as it progressed to its close. The Gwalior Contingent, which had hung like a threatening cloud over the Delhi Field Force, and which for such a period could have decided by a move the fate of the siege, and consequently of India, marched, when Delhi had fallen, and Lucknow had been relieved, and we heard of the fierce battle they had fought at Cawnpore, and afterwards of their total defeat by the commander-in-chief. It was by such acts of folly on the part of our enemy that we were saved in the great crisis. This war was begun by the *sepoys* in treachery, ingratitude and cruelty; was continued in ignorance and incapacity, without energy and without courage; and ended, without bringing to the surface one redeeming trait, or one man fit to rule.

The work carried on with most interest was the search for prize. Agents had been elected before the capture, and were diligently employed in gathering the booty, but the greater portion was lost through ignorance of its whereabouts.

They commenced by seizing the horses, carriages, and furniture—things that could not be concealed. The troops had entered the city calculating the booty at millions of *rupees*, but where these *rupees* were no one save the natives had an idea. The knowledge dawned on us when the greater part had been abstracted by those better informed. The *badmashes* knew the rich houses and where the coin was likely to be concealed, and they worked diligently in the dead of night. The prize agents employed a number of officers in the search. For a short period, it became a most exciting pursuit, and my husband was actively and successfully engaged. After an early breakfast, he would start, with a troop of *coolies*, armed with picks, crowbars, and measuring lines. A house said to contain treasure would be allotted for the day's proceedings, and the business would commence by a careful survey of the premises. The houses enclosed a large extent of ground, generally containing two or three courts.

The rooms faced on the courts, which were usually planted with grass, and shaded with shrubs. The houses seldom rose above one storey, with flat roofs, and staircases leading up to them, greatly facilitating the survey. By a careful measurement of the roofs above and of the rooms below, any concealed space could be detected. Then the walls were broken through, and if there was a secret room or a built-up niche or recess, it would be discovered, and some large prizes rewarded their search.

On one occasion I had asked a few friends to lunch, expecting Colonel Muter home, when a guest informed me there was no chance of his return as a large treasure he could not leave had been found. It was late when he came back with thirteen waggons loaded with spoil, and, among other valuables, eighty thousand *rupees*; in English money eight thousand pounds. On another occasion, after thoroughly ransacking a house and obtaining silver vessels and gold ornaments, before the party withdrew a *coolie* was directed to drive his pick into the grass of the court, and the first stroke went through a bag of a thousand *rupees*. Planted side by side in a neat border, under the earth, these bags were laid around the enclosure, but the canvas was so rotten and the night so dark that the work could not be finished, and it was not possible, without sleeping over the treasure, to preserve it to the agency.

Hours would be lost in detecting and digging from the *chunammed* floors ponderous iron boxes to find them empty; but the keenest disappointment arose from the way the city was plundered by those not working for the army. Days were spent in ascertaining where a treasure had been hid, only to learn that the prize was gone, most probably to some of the ruffians who had aided in the plunder of the cantonment, and who had imbrued their hands in the blood of the victims of Delhi. We heard rumours from time to time that some of the searchers among those no one would have suspected of the crime, had "annexed" to themselves articles of value, forgetful that all secured was expected to form a fund out of which the wounded, those invalided or in hospital from illness contracted in the campaign, were intended honourably to share.

In fact, in a recent work I was shocked to read that an officer openly confessed that "human nature "could not resist the temptation to appropriate valuable jewellery. All such would have done well to look up the Book of Joshua, seventh chapter, and read how loot was and is regarded by the All-seeing Eye. It did not save Achan to confess (verse 21):

When I saw among the spoils a goodly Babylonish garment, and two hundred shekels of silver, and a wedge of gold of fifty *shekels* weight, then I coveted them, and took them; and behold they are hid in the earth in the midst of my tent, and the silver under it.

The punishment accorded would in these days be considered terribly severe in proportion to the offence, inasmuch as it fell on all the family and possessions of Achan; but who are we to express our judgment? Shall not the Judge of all the earth do right?

The tent where the more valuable articles were displayed was pitched on the flat roof of a house overlooking the court of the *Dewan-Kass*. There were several iron strong boxes among a miscellaneous collection, bearing traces of having been buried; and on chairs, sofas, and tables were shawls, silks, kincobs, swords, daggers, fans, and fowling-pieces. A prize agent opened one of the iron chests, and I saw pearls, emeralds, rings, and jewellery of every kind. Glass was mixed with precious stones of great worth, and pearls that required a practised eye to detect they were false. A friend wrote to me from Meerut to ask if I could get her into the prize tent, as she wished to buy some pearls. I answered, "Certainly"—and she came.

We went together to the prize tent, and I introduced her as requiring some fine pearls. Some were shown her which she said were, to all appearance, what she wished, but she could not buy without testing.

What I will do will not injure them if sound; but, if false, they will be destroyed. I have brought a needle with me which I would insert into the hole drilled through the pearl and try to work it about. If the pearl is genuine no harm will result, but, if false, if will be destroyed.

Permission granted, my friend inserted her needle, and as she worked it these fine pearls proved to be clever imitations in wax with a fine glaze over.

Often there was something paltry in the richest ornament. In a crown of pure gold, found by my husband in the palace of the empress, there were drops of green glass to represent emeralds. Silver vessels were sold for their weight in *rupees*, and at this rate an officer of the *carabiniers* purchased a massive tea-pot of spurious metal under the impression that it was silver. The native jewellery was pure in metal, but uncouth in form; diamonds and emeralds large but flat; and although they excel at Delhi in filigree work, and can copy English patterns, yet the setting of these jewels was generally very coarse.

I was much interested in a collection of miniatures and portraits of Europeans found during the search. Many had belonged to the murdered, and the agents wished them to be recognised and returned to those who valued them. There were Bibles and prayer-books, with the names of ladies who had perished on the fly-leaf. And neither the palace of the king nor the house of the queen was exempt from these relics, which so strongly condemned them.

The Great *Mogul* was now our prisoner and lodged in a small house within the palace. Shortly after Delhi fell the royal family had been captured and brought in by Major Hodson. He had shot on the spot two of the king's sons and a grandson. The eldest of these princes was a fine young man, the grandson a mere stripling; but if half the stories told of this boy were true, he was one of the most depraved monsters nursed by the Mutiny.

Enough was elicited on the king's trial to show how dissipated and reckless these young men had been. Instead of leading in the field the revolted regiments that had proclaimed their father emperor, they

MAHOMED SURAJ-OO-DEEN SHAH GAZEE
Titular King of Delhi

headed the Mutiny only in its murders and in its outrages. The petitions of the people for protection, and the records of the siege kept by the natives, prove that though they shrank from no unlawful act, they recoiled with fear and trembling from meeting our army in battle. The bodies of these ill-fated young men were carried to Delhi, and exposed in the Chandnee Chowk.

It was remarkable how fatal this Mutiny was to all who took a leading part in it—to us as well as to the enemy. Nearly every native prince or noble who led in the war against us either fell in battle, or perished by the hand of the executioner, and the number of our own leaders who were killed in the field, or sank under the fatigues of the campaign, has been a subject of deep grief to the nation. The sentence on the king was banishment for life to Burmah. He was permitted to take Zenud Mahal with him and five sons.

A commission was sitting for the trial of native prisoners of rank, and the *Nawab* of Jugghur and the *Rajah* of Bolubghur had already perished by its sentence. The estates of these gentlemen lay on the Agra side of Delhi, in a district wholly in the hands of the rebels. The choice between the English who might again come into power, and the mutineers who were in power, was one of great difficulty to natives acting without fixed principles, and inclining to that side they expected to be most to their advantage. For months the scales had been evenly balanced; the prestige of empire was with us, but the belief throughout the land was that our sway had ended. With them the essence of politics is to temporise, and they had no true conception of the character of their rulers.

From their infancy they had been accustomed to the mild government of England, and they looked at the worst for interminable law proceedings. Acting on this conviction, at the same time that they furnished the King of Delhi with the sinews of war, they endeavoured to keep up a communication with the English general. Unfortunately for them, when the king deserted his palace, he left evidence strewed about sufficient to convict them—papers that told a strange tale. That such proof against his supporters, which he had ample time to destroy, should have been left open and exposed was a remarkable act. Similar instances occurred during the war, and furnish another of the unaccountable proceedings of this unaccountable people.

The *nawab* was in Delhi when the mutineers entered from Meerut, and he was much blamed for not aiding our people with his numerous followers. He replied to this with startling justice that:

It was England who had armed and trained the ruffians who had brought the calamity on the land; and it was not fair to expect him to compel that obedience in his followers which the rulers of the country and his judges had failed in compelling among their own.

This prince met his fate on the gallows with a calmness, a fortitude, and gentlemanly bearing that inspired my husband, who commanded the escort, with the deepest respect.

More melancholy still was the death of the *rajah*, whose sympathies as a Hindoo were probably as much with the English as with the Moslem emperor. Gentle in manner, young and handsome in person, it was the hard fate of this noble to be placed in circumstances wherein every path was fraught with peril and to be tried when death was the award of any act hostile to our rule. There was something touching in the last words he spoke before his judges:

I was securely seated on a goodly bough of a flourishing tree, and my own act has sawn asunder the branch on which I rested.

The king's turn had come to appear before this fatal tribunal, and all were anxious to see how the old man would deport himself on the trying occasion. The commission sat in the *Dewan-Kass*—that private hall of reception sacred to him, and which the etiquette of the court for centuries had forbidden any to enter except by command. Not often even in history has such an instance of the vanity of human power been seen as when this representative of one of the greatest houses was arraigned for high crimes before a few British officers—not one of whom held the substantive commission of lieutenant-colonel.

As he was borne through the arch of the inner court, the unhappy sovereign might have observed two cleverly executed outlines in chalk on the wall of the recess, which in the days of his prosperity the guard nearest his person had occupied. Both were so strikingly like his sharp aquiline face and attenuated form that the words written beneath were unnecessary to convey to anyone who had seen him the meaning of the drawings: "The King of Delhi as he is," was under the first; the others represented him hanging from a gibbet, and beneath it was written: "The King of Delhi as he ought to be."

I was present at the proceedings, which were opened by an able and eloquent address from the judge advocate-general, in which he spoke to the charges against the king. The trial was one of investigation, and the Court would come to a finding, but had no power

139

to pass sentence. They would record evidence, now the opportunity offered, that would eventually be of great historical interest, besides determining how far the king was really culpable.

Then the fallen monarch appeared under an escort of riflemen, and his *palanquin* was carried into the hall. He was accompanied by Jumma Buckt, the child of his old age and of his wife Zenud Mahal, now almost the only survivor that remained to him of his family. Before him sat the commission by whose stern sentence so many of that family had already perished, and the guards around him wore the uniform of the soldiers beneath whose bullets they had fallen. The feeble old man rested on a pile of cushions on the floor. He was short in stature, and of a slight, infirm figure; his face was handsomely cut, the nose prominent and aquiline, the features intelligent, and with an air of refinement that did not disgrace his high descent.

The trial had been postponed from week to week by his illness, and was now delayed by frequent adjournments to give him time for repose. At first, he appeared alarmed, and his face wore an anxious expression; but by degrees it became more vacant, and he assumed or felt indifference, remaining apparently in a state of lethargy, with his eyes closed during the greater part of the proceedings.

One of the chief questions was, whether the king had sanctioned the murder of the Christians who had escaped the first massacres; and I believe the commission found that his order for the execution had been obtained. It appeared from what I gathered that he had condemned the conduct of the *nana* at Cawnpore; and there was abundant proof that he had striven hard to protect the citizens of Delhi from the violence of the soldiery and the outrages of the nobles, and the people in the country from the plundering *Goojurs*.

It was clear how wretched the old man had been when eddied about in the whirlwind of the Mutiny with no energy to control, and no force of will to rule the cruel natures around. Numerous petitions from the people were translated, with the king's remarks. Much of what he said was sound and good, but his complaints were bitter of the insolence of the *sepoys*, who had so cringed to us. How keenly he felt the thorns in the bed which had been prepared for him! He was a mere puppet who had drifted down a stream and suddenly found itself the most prominent object in a vast sea of trouble.

I cannot think that in the treatment of the last of the house of Timour our country showed her usual liberality. We must keep the fact ever before us, that it was our army that set the country in a

ZENAT MAHAL-BEGUM, OR QUEEN OF DELHI

blaze—that it was our timidity that led to the great catastrophe; and we have not even the excuse that the Mutiny was an unforeseen event.

Some weeks before the outbreak my husband repeated a conversation he had held with Mr. Hodson, afterwards the celebrated leader of "Hodson's Horse," who said:—

> Some years ago, I was at a public dinner given to a Governor-General of India. In drinking his health an allusion was made to the campaign on the Sutlej, and in reply he observed; 'Trust me, gentlemen, your greatest war is to come, and that will be with your own Native Army.' Mr. Hodson added: 'I was even then impressed with the truth of this remark, and I now believe the predicted war is drawing near.'

A few months only elapsed when that good soldier himself fell in the conflict he had foreseen.

Amid all the poverty and contempt thrown on the king, I was gratified to observe the demeanour of many of the witnesses when called to give evidence. Bowing to the ground with hands clasped, before the miserable figure on the bed, addressed by them as "Ruler of the Universe," though by the committee as *tum* (pronounced "toom": a mode of address only used to inferiors and servants) they observed to the powerless old man a degree of respect denied to the Court, who had only to nod the signal for their execution. The demeanour of young Jumma Buckt, on the trial of his father, was an exhibition of bad taste, and in striking contrast to that of the old servant who attended the king.

The residence of the empress in the days of her prosperity was situated in the city, at some distance from the palace. The house is a fair specimen of the dwellings of the grandees in Delhi, and one day I accompanied my husband to inspect the mansion. Part of the building stood on the street, three storeys high. I passed under an archway by outhouses into a passage leading into an oblong court with buildings facing me around. A canal ran through the centre of the court, with the usual fountains, and the ground was laid out as a garden.

The buildings were one-storeyed, with a flat roof; a row of rooms opened to the court, and another row was behind them. The apartments of the queen were at the ends of the parallelogram, tastefully decorated. A large portion of the prize had been taken in this house, and in the search the agents had turned it upside down. Broken china strewed the floors, torn drapery and articles of little value covered the court, piles of earth showed where holes had been dug, and walls with great openings dashed through them proved that no difficulties had stood in the way. By a side door I went into a smaller court, and from that into another, no two of them alike. Then I came to a range of outhouses and of stabling. The extent was considerable, though the accommodation was not great.

The *Jumma Musjid* holds the same rank in India that St. Peter's does in the Roman Catholic world. Like St. Paul's, it stands in the heart of the city on slightly rising ground. The plateau from which the walls arise is a stupendous structure, and the steps and gateway are worthy of the plateau. When there, the visitor is in a vast open court, paved with blocks of sandstone—the material of the building, excepting the domes and minarets, which are composed of marble. From one of the tall spires he looks over the country as from an aeroplane, and like a novice at the masthead he wonders how the slight column can bear him aloft. The old ruins around Delhi away to the Kootub, eleven miles off, are visible from this spot.

Delhi was a great city before the Moslem set his foot in Hindostan, and for ages it has swayed backwards and forwards on the banks of the Jumna within range of this view. Upon a rocky soil, plentifully supplied with stone, many traces must remain of so ancient a city; and ruins are everywhere to be found, of which the most remarkable is the Kootub. This exquisite tower, like the Taj at Agra, is the most perfect work of its kind; but the tower is so old, and its history so obscure, that it loses much of the interest attaching to the mausoleum. The summit of that tower, from which I also gazed, has its own story of the Mutiny; for some of the retreating *sepoys*, who there sought refuge, were hurled from the top.

With the first of the year, officers began to arrive from England, and again communication was opened along the great military road. As yet, however, it was only the Doab that was cleared of the muti-neers, for all the country on the left bank of the Ganges was in arms, and there was little but rebellion on the right bank of the Jumna.

The battalion received its orders to march to Meerut on February 1st, 1858. The bundles of our servants had greatly increased, and their demand for carriage was now on a most extravagant scale. The bearer (Colonel Muter's personal attendant) had been of great service during the Mutiny, but of late had been found impossible to move; he had taken up his residence in a room at the foot of our entrance steps, and he feared to leave the spot, where he kept watch over his plunder. The

The Kootub Minar on Ruins of Old Delhi

cares of riches were now embarrassing him, and the robber dreaded being robbed. Having a wholesome fear of the prize agents, he did not appear in kincobs and satins till after his return to Meerut; but then— he turned out in princely costume. Grandeur such as his could not be expected to work, so he passed away like a comet, and I bethought me of the old saying, "*It is an ill wind that blows nobody good.*"

Part 3: Hot Weather Campaign in Rohilcund

CHAPTER 8

The road from the palace was lined with the gallant little Goorkhas as the Rifles passed out on their return to Meerut, and the chilly air rang with the cheers of their old companions in arms.

At this time rest was unknown in India, the country being in commotion with moving columns and the war, hitherto local, was more general throughout the land. It is seldom that so wide a field of operations has been seen, and it was necessary to make up by constant movement for the want of numbers, though a stream of troops had been poured into Hindostan by both the sea and overland routes.

We had scarcely settled in our old house before a wing of the 60th joined a force under General Penny in the march to Kassgunje and my husband left Meerut in command of the Rifles, when I was once more alone. But life in the cantonment was now greatly changed from the days when he had gone to the Siege of Delhi. Scarcely a trace remained of the fortifications, and though gloom still hung over the *bazaars*, the roads were again gay with carriages, and the station had returned to its pristine ways.

It is difficult, perhaps impossible, for those who live at home at ease fully to realise the relief a feeling of security brings. Every day blessings are the greatest though least appreciated till lost, and there are many the full value of which can never be known in Great Britain, for I believe our country to be so constituted that they can never be lost. During the weary months I had passed in Meerut how ardently I longed to enjoy an existence free from this weight of danger, this depressing, never-ceasing apprehension of a dreadful fate felt during the day and during the night, asleep and awake; a sword suspended over the head, embittering every enjoyment of life. Often my imagination carried me far from this distracted land and pictured the happiness of an English fireside, of home and safety.

Although this absolute security was denied, still I contrasted with thankfulness the comparative freedom from danger both of the English in these Provinces, and of the service in which the troops were engaged. Before, under a scorching sun, the men, isolated, far in Asia among hosts of enemies, had gone forth to a task of desperation; now the rebellion had been met, checked, rolled back, and the voice of encouragement, of sympathy and of assistance, came with an earnest sound from our country, and met an eager welcome.

In the interval of my husband's absence, the joyous news reached me that he was named for the command of one of the Convalescent Depots on the Himalayah Mountains; but the appointment was not to be taken up until the service required from the battalion had been completed. It soon appeared that the commander-in-chief had views for the 60th incompatible with the detachment of the wing under General Penny. That wing was directed to march on Roorkee, the great Engineer station, where a strong force had been for some time assembling. Then the commander-in-chief's plan was made known to our colonel, who was ordered to march the remainder of the battalion to Roorkee and assume command of the column now designated "The Roorkee Field Force." At the same time, he was gazetted a Brigadier-General, and desired to select a staff, when he named my husband his D.A. Adjutant-General.

The proceedings of this force will afford my readers more interest than a detail of the stupid life I led at Meerut; and I therefore give a general idea of the campaign that followed, gained from letters, telegrams, and despatches.

The Roorkee Field Force crossed the Ganges and entered Rohilcund below the pilgrim city of Hurdwan, where the clear stream debouches from the hills, and hurries over a stony bed into the alluvial soil of the plains.

Along the foot of the Himalayah runs a belt of forest land inundated in the rainy season, and always covered with a tropical vegetation— a region of fever and a den of wild beasts. In droves the towering elephant crushes down the underwood, the crouching tiger hides in the thickest lairs, and the screech of the hyena and the howls of wolves and of jackals are heard without cessation through the night. In so fit a region were enacted some of the tragedies of these terrible times.

147

The advancing footsteps of the British Army pressed back the native troops into the wilderness, and the *Nana*, with many of the leaders and a crowd of followers, is said to have perished there from the deadly effect of the climate.

From Hurdwan the Ganges takes a wide bend, enclosing between its waters and the ranges of the Himalayah the country forming the provinces of Rohilcund and of Oude. This tract is, perhaps, the fairest in India. The great mountains that rear their icy crests along its length roll many streams through its plains to the sacred river—plains level as a bowling green and fertile as those of Lombardy. With the exception of the belt I have described it is well cultivated, and covered with goodly cities.

Such were the newly acquired kingdom of Oude and our old province of Rohilcund, where the Mutiny erected its strongholds, and whence it drew its chief strength.

When the Doab had been cleared, and the right bank of the Ganges was in our hands, Sir Colin Campbell (afterwards Lord Clyde) placed a cordon from the hills at Hurdwan to the territory of Nepaul, and having fixed his nets, he drew in his prey. The rebels had the option of retiring into the belt I have described, called the Terai, or of breaking through his lines; but neither course held out much hope of escape. It was in reality death from disease, or death by the sword that was offered.

The columns were put simultaneously into motion, and although acting many hundreds of miles apart, the movements were so directed that they converged together on the city of Bareilly about the central spot.

General Jones's force was, therefore, not an independent column, but a portion of an army acting on the enemy's flank, and one skilfully handled by His Excellency, and ably directed by its commander. It was required to sweep the land from the point where the river cuts through the Terai, while General Penny held a post in the centre, and Sir Colin, in command of a splendid force, advanced from the southeast. The fords of the Ganges were well guarded. As the Roorkee Field Force came down from the north-west, His Excellency drew up from the south-east, and as they closed General Penny crossed the river and pushed on to the capital.

The enemy, distracted by the advancing dangers, offered no combined resistance. Khan Bahadoor Khan, who reigned at Bareilly, only attempted to stop Sir Colin's advance when his guns were within

General Sir Colin Campbell GCB

reach of the city, and he was then totally defeated. General Penny was killed on his march from the river to join the commander-in-chief.

But the most successful of these columns was that under Brigadier-General John Jones, who proudly boasted no gun was pointed at him that he did not capture, and who inflicted so signal a punishment on the mutineers that he received in India the *sobriquet* of "the Avenger."

When the Roorkee Field Force crossed the Ganges, it entered the Terai; and here the enemy committed one of those many mistakes made by the Sepoys which prove that however defective may have been our own intelligence theirs was still worse.

It was some time before the material could be collected for throwing a bridge across the river, and a small party was detached from Roorkee to guard the men engaged in the work. The enemy moved a force through the forest from a ford they held in strength opposite the city of Nujeebabad, probably to demolish both the party and the work. In the centre of the Terai they came in contact with the column, in full march to attack their position, and the shock was fatal to the rebels. They lost all their material and left hundreds in the thickets to be devoured by wild beasts. The prestige of the rebellion also, in these parts, was destroyed. The natives, who would not believe a simple truth, who were ignorant of passing events to an inconceivable extent, and credited an enemy's success only when he was at their door, saw the men who had so long boasted of their prowess emerge from the forest in a panic, without arms, and many even without clothes.

No attempt was made to defend Nujeebabad. The *nawab* fled from his palace, which was destroyed, and his strong fort surrendered without a blow.

Before the troops had passed through the deserted city, the camp-followers, like a swarm of noxious insects, had darted on their prey. In a short time, the town and the surrounding country were in flames, and the general beheld with dismay the first results of his operations in the destruction of the fair country he had entered. He seemed to have let loose on the unhappy land a legion of fiends; but he had the power to bind as well as to loose, and the energetic measures adopted saved the province.

English people can scarcely believe in the wickedness of actual war. Its civilised and legitimate operations are terrible enough, but without an iron hand to repress, there is no cruelty, no crime, however dreadful, that will not be enacted under its shade. The first day's operations left a crowd of wounded to an awful death; the next two or three saw a city deserted and destroyed, the villages around in a blaze, and the country covered with men as ready to murder as to steal; and bent on destruction. If the extermination of the province were aimed at, the general had but to protect the plunderer, and without the aid of a soldier the land throughout its length and breadth would have become a howling wilderness. Some of the dreadful men who perpetrated these enormities stole away from the ranks of the army; numbers came from among its followers, but the country itself furnished the most—and, I fear, this would be true of most countries.

Between Nujeebabad and Moradabad is a town called Nugeena, with a canal flowing in its front. The enemy fell back on it, and from the fords of the Ganges and the country around their troops assembled, and drew up between Nugeena and the canal to dispute the passage of the field force. The general heard with pleasure that his enemies were gathering together, and waited a few days, both to give them time and to allow his siege-train to be carried across the ford from Roorkee.

At midnight on April 21st the British troops got under arms, and about eight o'clock the advance guard passed over the bridge of the canal. The head of the column halted on the bridge, the horses were taken from the guns to water, and the men fell out for a few minutes. In the meantime, the advance guard turned to the right and pursued its way along the bank of the canal. It was not aware that the main body had halted, as it was hidden by a belt of trees that lined the canal. A vedette far on the left flank brought in the intelligence that the enemy were in force in front, on the flank, and stretching for more than a mile opposite the road the advance guard had passed over, but they were concealed in the *topees* (groves of trees) that grew so thickly around Nugeena.

The guard was now in considerable danger, as the column had not yet crossed; but the news set the force into rapid motion, and, with such practised soldiers, a few minutes only were required to place it in line of battle. Then the enemy's guns opened, but they opened only to give points of attack to the different regiments moving swiftly on. It was now discovered that a heavy battery actually commanded the bridge, and that the rebels had lost another of the many chances offered by the fortune of war of inflicting on us serious loss. It was said they were late in taking up their position, and the general earlier in the field than could have been expected, which may have been the case, as he had already marched some fourteen miles. It is, however, a fact, that though they often did foolishly desperate acts, they still more frequently failed to take the most favourable opportunities.

Rapidity of movement was now economy of life, and each regiment swept on to its attack with a speed that left the artillery little time for action and dispersed the rebel force as chaff before the wind.

Short as this action was, it was sufficiently fatal to the men of Rohilcund. More than a thousand of them were killed on the field, all their guns were taken, the city was occupied, and none dared thereafter openly to dispute the march of "the Avenger."

The column quickly advanced on Moradabad, which the rebels as hastily evacuated. Nearly all the local leaders of influence were captured in that city, and the chief of them was at once shot to prevent the possibility of a rescue. The next day the bodies of the others swung from a long gibbet in the centre of the beautiful little cantonment they had so desolated.

As the force moved on, the enemy abandoned the forts on its left, and the fords of the river on its right; and thus, relieved the Doab from the pressure the presence of the mutineers had kept up on our side, while the fugitives went flocking in thousands to Bareilly.

In vain Khan Bahadoor Khan sent out a general to check the progress of the column. The latter made a display with his cavalry, but the brigadier-general's irregulars, supported by a squadron of Dragoon Guards, stole round to his flank, then charged, and he was driven in at full gallop, with the loss of all his guns and, it is said, of his own life.

Already the commander-in-chief was nearing Bareilly, the capital, and the short space between the approaching columns was densely occupied by those whose black deeds placed them beyond the pale of forgiveness. The traitor Khan now trembled for his existence, notwithstanding the countenance and support of that determined miscreant, the Lucknow *moulvie*, and of that infamous monster, the *nana*, who is reported to have said to the cowering chief, "It is as well to be drowned with a foot of water over your head as with an inch."

It was not water, however, that was to finish the career of the *khan*; he was destined to be hanged, and although he managed for years to evade this fate, yet the day came when he died on a gibbet in the capital he had ruled—boasting when he saw there was no hope of mercy, of his own excesses and of the number of *Kaffirs* his orders had consigned to Jehanum.

The brigadier-general strove unsuccessfully to obtain tidings of the movements of the commander-in-chief. Messenger after messenger was despatched with promise of large reward if one of them succeeded in bringing a reply to the little piece of paper rolled up in a quill, but no reply came. The country swarmed with the enemy's cavalry. The brigadier-general, confident in his own force, dashed straight at the town, and on the day following that when Sir Colin defeated Khan Bahadoor Khan some seven miles from Bareilly, the Roorkee Field Force, pushing back all opposition, entered the city, and, fighting its way through the streets, gained the centre, and there occupied and barricaded the principal buildings.

Then the shells from the other column fell crashing through the roofs of these houses, so that the forces actually came in contact before their proximity could be ascertained. Three men of the Rifles passed over the deserted streets till they emerged at the opposite end of the town, where they beheld in long lines of tents the immense array of His Excellency's force. The junction was then complete, but the nest of great traitors was gone—the *nana*, the *khan*, and the *moulvie*,—all had fled, and the torrent pent up between the approaching columns had poured round the flank of the chief, and inundated his rear.

★★★★★★

The experiences of the column under the commander-in chief, Sir Colin Campbell, afterwards Lord Clyde, are fully detailed in the second volume of *My Diary in India*, by Dr. Russell, the *Times* correspondent. Published in two volumes by George Routledge & Sons, Broadway House, Ludgate Hill, London, 1860.

★★★★★★

The difficulty was to deal with the numerous horsemen that formed the chief strength of the revolted province, and while Sir Colin was operating against Bareilly, they were threatening the posts along the line of his communication, had recaptured Shahjehanpore, and were shelling the garrison which had taken refuge in the gaol.

The Roorkee Field Force was broken up, and the brigadier-general, with his staff, was appointed to one of still greater strength to march as quickly as possible to the relief of this garrison.

The atmosphere was now heated to the temperature of a burning furnace—a heat those only can understand who have experienced it. I will not dwell on a subject Mr. Russell's graphic pen has described, who then learned, in common with the newly arrived soldiers, what the withering effects of a hot-weather campaign in India really are.

The relief was effected and Shahjehanpore occupied, but the enemy assembled in great masses in front of the town, and his cavalry rode freely over the country. More than once he attacked the position, and a portion of his horse actually burst into the cantonment through the force drawn out, and were cut up or dispersed in the rear.

After the chief had completed the arrangements for the occupation of Rohilcund, he passed through Shahjehanpore with a strong escort, remaining there a few days. He had scarcely arrived when the *moulvie*, who commanded the opposing forces, and was more soldier than priest, attacked him. One shot nearly finished his career, passing between him and the now celebrated chief of the staff.

The greater portion of the escort was left with the brigadier-general, who was further reinforced by a brigade of Punjaub troops, under a tried and able leader, and he received orders to drive the rebels through Mahumdee back into the Terai.

The sun rose, on the morning of May 24th, on the glittering line with which the general swept the country. No power in Asia could for a moment, on such a plain, have borne the shock of such a force; and the enemy, like a swarm of bees buzzing thickly before and around the flanks, vanished from its front.

The sun did what the rebels could not do; it filled the hospitals and strewed the rear with dead. Mahumdee was taken, the fort destroyed, and the enemy scattered; so, the general withdrew to Shahjehanpore, the field force was broken up, and the troops retired into quarters from the deadly sun, now acting with a force that even the most seasoned could not withstand.

Part 4: The Murree Hills

CHAPTER 9

A military body on active service requires a much more extensive staff than the same troops in quarters. When the field force therefore returned it was at once broken up, and my husband was at liberty to take up the appointment to which he had been nominated.

Under other circumstances such a journey would not have been undertaken; the heat was appalling, the distance more than a thousand miles. But the temptation was irresistible. The imagination revelled amid cool breezes on the snowy heights near the fairy region of Cashmere, and I received an intimation that Colonel Muter would at once commence his return. My "marching orders" were most laconic:—

> Sell off furniture and effects at once. Despatch without delay to Murree by hackery all things indispensable there; go to hotel. Have all ready to start when I arrive. Order for me hot bath, fresh clothing; also, dinner for two; lay *dak* (post carriage) to start on journey half-hour after dinner. Do the best you can. I shall be satisfied.

On receiving this programme, I went to my dear friend Mrs. Palmer, wife of Colonel Palmer, C.B., of the 60th Rifles, to consult together as the time was so short in which to do so much. "Before we go further," she said, "you must at once come to us. We live so close that we shall both have some amusement with your auction." "That will suit me admirably; now I will send for the sergeant in the artillery, who, I am told, is a first-rate auctioneer."

I did so. I took him over our bungalow, with which he seemed pleased, and so many things were nice and pretty, besides being so abnormally clean and in good order, that he prognosticated good results.

"But," I remarked, "there is no time for proper announcement?" I will 'lot' this afternoon, and begin sale tomorrow morning."

Next, I got packers under our *khansamah* and my *ayah* to pack our clothing to send off by bullock-carts next day, and, fairly tired, went to Mrs. Palmer to rest and report. I told her the "important sale" was to begin early next morning, as the fact would be proclaimed to the station by the beating of *tum-tums*.

I was so excited by the coming event that my slumbers were disturbed, so I was quite prepared for the "amusement "my dear friend had anticipated when the call to business sounded. As we were only separated by the Mall from our compound, though the trees and shrubs interposed, so that we could not see the people; yet we could hear them, and the hum of voices and the rumble of wheels, of conveyances of every class, told of a large attendance, and proclaimed that no small stir was in progress.

At the close of the day's work my auctioneer-sergeant came over to me with his bags of *rupees* and said he had never witnessed such a sale. There was no "alarming sacrifice" to us, or "big bargains" for the purchasers. He said the people struggled to secure the things. The fires and destruction of every description incurred during the dark first days of the Mutiny had caused a famine in furniture and household effects. A little carriage and pair of ponies my dear husband had given me fetched three times the cost to him, and, altogether, the result, in up-to-date parlance, constituted a "record."

I was confident Colonel Muter would consider I had carried out his directions "to do the best I could," though I was a simple spectator and unable to exert any influence for or against.

On his way back, as well as on the march from Hurdwan, my husband passed through three ruined cantonments of no ordinary beauty. Each had its tragic story, and each presented a type of the senseless and wanton destruction that marked the career of the mutineers. Of these the most tragic and the most beautiful was that of Shahjehanpore.

The station lay behind the city, both standing on a tongue of land between two rivers, the latter occupying the spot where the waters of these streams met. A pretty church had been erected in the centre of the ground allotted to the military. It was a ruin, memorable for one of the most bloodthirsty deeds of this miserable revolt.

From Moradabad the English rode to Meerut; from Bareilly many got away to Nynee-tal, but from Shahjehanpore there was no escape.

It was in that church, when the victims were assembled to worship God, that the crime was perpetrated. It was on His altar the blood of

His people fell. Could any look unmoved on such a spot? Is it surprising that both the governor-general and the commander-in-chief strove in vain to restrain the thirst for vengeance, and that a word for mercy and forgiveness stamped the utterer "a white pandy"? It was with a savage delight the artillery pitched their shells into the deserted city, and many officers with secret satisfaction saw a whole quarter of the town in flame.

I had forwarded the things reserved from the sale of our furniture by that useful institution, the Government bullock vans. Immediately on my husband's return, as all was ready, we left Meerut on a journey I shall never forget, doing our first stage to Delhi on June 8th, 1858.

The first portion of the road we traversed in *gharries*, but much the greater part was by *palkee dak*, that is, borne on the shoulders of *coolies*.

During the night we travelled, resting at the Travellers' Bungalows when the sun had set. In every country where travelling is the most primitive, it is, at the same time, most uncomfortable, expensive, and slow. A change has come over India, and with railways and comfortable hotels a traveller now can scarcely comprehend the wretched way in which we were compelled to travel from Umballa to Murree.

Up to Umballa the road was complete, and the little pony dragged on the heavy, clumsy *gharry* at a considerable pace over the smooth, level road; but from this station our troubles commenced, and the farther north we got the worse and more unmanageable the bearers became. I often heard them discussing the great topic of the day, and generally they expressed doubts of our success at Delhi. Indeed, on one occasion, I had to pull back the curtains of my *palkee* and assure them the Mutiny was crushed, and that I had been present at the trial of the king in the *Dewan-Kass* at Delhi. For a time, this produced silence, though I am afraid not conviction. Their idea was that the Empire was still in jeopardy, and, native-like, their demeanour was objectionable in proportion.

As I feared to be left behind, I directed my *palkee* to be carried in front. Often it was with difficulty that the relays of bearers could be procured, and the sun would rise before we could reach our shelter, and light up the white road and baked plain with an intolerable glare. When it reached any height, our frail coverings seemed to curl and crack, while the rays struck upon the parched earth with a dazzling reflection, which a person in the strongest health could scarcely endure.

I was grieved to see that my husband's health had suffered severely from the effects of the two hot-weather campaigns. The terrible exposure in Rohilcund had followed too quickly on that before Delhi. An intermittent fever and ague seized him with a strong hold. His head had been "covered in the day of battle," but the sun had done what the enemy had been withheld from doing. It is often so with soldiers who, supported by the excitement of a campaign, will suffer more from disease when the work ceases than during the actual operations.

We had gone half the way when I began to doubt the wisdom of having undertaken the journey. Hitherto I had lived in a well-cooled bungalow during the hot weather, and I had no idea of the task we were undertaking when I first started. One morning, when day broke, I looked behind for my husband's *palkee* along the straight, monotonous road which I could trace away to the horizon. Surprised there was no *palkee* in sight, I despatched a messenger with a note to learn the cause and awaited his arrival in a *serai*. It was hours before mv husband came, and then in a native cart. He told me the *coolies* had deserted and left his *palkee* in the road, where it would have been death to remain. He had, therefore, left it, and took the opportunity of a native cart to proceed. Desiring me to follow, he continued his way to Umritsir.

When I re-entered my *palkee* all the bearers had vanished, and though I had waited for hours, it was now that they began to eat and to smoke. When they resumed the journey, the sun was high, and they suffered so much that at every well I was left on the burning highway till they had quenched their thirst. It was near the meridian when I reached the *dak* bungalow; the paint was burnt off the palanquin, and no words could describe the heat which this morning passed the endurance of nature, for dense clouds gathering burst into torrents of rain, and the earth trembled beneath the roar of the thunder.

As I expected, I found my husband suffering from an attack of fe-ver, and the doctor, an old friend who came to see us, advised him to proceed with all speed to the hills. When we started that night, I told the bearers, as the *Sahib* was ill, we must reach Lahore before sunrise, and for extra speed they should receive double *baksheesh*. At the first stage they were an hour over time, so I refused the extra amount, and directed them to carry on the invalid, who was asleep beyond the jabber of the altercation. The new *coolies* refused to proceed until the old ones had received the promised reward, and they all sat down in a circle, and passed round the hubble-bubble, whilst I in despair could see the torches of the other *palkee* in the distance as it was borne away.

A native on horseback, wearing the government badge, passed, and

I asked his assistance; but he replied these people had become so independent, not to say insolent, since the Mutiny that it would be useless for him to interfere, and that my only plan was to give the sum they demanded, which I was compelled to do. He also hinted it was not quite safe for us to travel without an escort as guard; especially as the *Sahib* was ill, and for most of the time weary and asleep. I carried also in my *palkee* all the money necessary for the journey, so on every account of safety it was imperative that we should not be separated.

On this journey we crossed the Sutlej, the Ravee, the Beas, the Chenab, and the Jhelum—the five rivers which give their combined names to the province, (Punjaub, or Five Rivers). Between the two last lies the plain where the Seikhs made their final stand against the British. My husband, who had been present in the battle, pointed out the ground where the power of this warlike sect had been broken under the walls of Goojerat.

The difference between the fighting qualities of the Seikhs and the Bengal *sepoys* was strikingly displayed in the campaigns of the Sutlej and Punjaub, and those of the Mutiny. The best contested actions fought in India were on those fields. There was something noble in the fair and open ground taken by the old Khalsa Army. They massed their troops and came boldly into the clear plains, inviting pitched battles; and when beaten after several of the bloodiest encounters since Waterloo, they surrendered. Like Cromwell's Ironsides on the return of Charles II., they took to honest agriculture, leaving the victorious army staggered by their losses and full of admiration for the prowess of their foes.

I awoke in the night after I had crossed the field of Goojerat from a dream that I was in a goodly ship on my passage home. The ripple of water and the splash of oars sounded in my ears. I looked abroad over a wide expanse of sea, and I thought my dream was true; but I was only on the mighty stream that drains the valley of Cashmere—the great and rapid Jhelum. I was in the route of the armies that from time immemorial had thus passed to the conquest of India. It was here that Porus had vainly attempted to stop the march of Alexander; and during the many centuries that had since elapsed several conquerors had pursued the same path, till our own great nation had turned the tide in the opposite direction and the victorious armies now moved from the plains of Hindustan.

Some years before Sir Walter Gilbert lost many of his camp-followers while fording this stream in his quick pursuit of the Afghan and Punjaub forces, when he was accompanied by the 60th Rifles, in which my husband was then a lieutenant.

Hitherto this journey had been over a country without a hill except where the land rose beyond the Jhelum, and was broken by the most extraordinary ruts and chasms. It seemed as if the surface had been level, and heavy rains had torn it up, leaving it intersected after a series of deluges with innumerable gigantic watercourses. The old road from the town of Jhelum led for some thirty miles through one of these passes, and close to its entrance is situated one of those forts of stupendous walls which are so often seen in the Mahratta country. This was Bakralla Pass and the Fort of Rotass.

Now I was about to enter the region of hills where my imagination had not ceased to dwell, the thought of which had sustained me during that fatiguing time, and which was to reward me for all the trials of that fearful road.

From the bungalow at Rawul-Pindee I looked up to the dark line of mountains where the station of Murree stood; and it was with indescribable pleasure I entered the palkee for the last time. There was a change in the dress and appearance of the bearers—even the mode of carrying the palanquin was different. I saw this at a glance, I felt it in the motion, I heard it in the grunts by which the bearers relieve the monotony of their toilsome stage.

CHAPTER 10

I awoke as my bearers placed my *palkee* under the verandah of the Trete Dak bungalow, and I felt I was in another atmosphere.

The bungalow stood on a projection in the centre of a long valley, in which I could trace the road winding among the trees in the hollows, and coming out on the bare sides of the projections, till it was lost beyond the tower at the top, with nothing but the clear sky behind it. The sides of the valley low down were cut in terraces, like flights of steps, all glittering with an inundation of water. These were rice-fields; cottages were grouped here and there in the queerest and most improbable places, standing out like large boulders from the rocky sides of the mountain.

A stream ran rapidly down the dark hollow beneath, and circled round the projection where I stood. The road I had come up was cut along a precipice down to the stream, which it crossed by a mountain bridge, and both it and the water were lost in the black gorge far below. The mountains reared their majestic sides so near that I could not see their tops. Here they were wooded, there green with grass, and anon piled up with frowning rocks. Everything was changed around me—the vegetation, the aspect of Nature, and the climate.

Seldom have I felt happier than when borne up this hill to the picturesque station of Murree. I regarded the scene as one regards a prize which has cost hard toil to gain. Gurgling streams came sparkling down the slopes with a sound sweeter than music. Imagination carried me back to the days of my childhood, and, in fancy, I was again in an English dell with trickling water rolling over the mossy stones. I could not resist the inclination to walk where the towering mountain gave me shade or the branches of the forest broke the rays of the sun. This is regarded by the bearers as a cabman would regard a fare who insisted on getting into the street and running after the cab.

I passed a pretty garden, and was gracefully presented with a bouquet of flowers by a little boy. This act augured well for the feeling of the hill people.

As we approached the summit the hateful sound of cannon rumbled from above, and I could see where the balls struck. The target was placed close by a cutting on the hillside, which marked the course of the road, and we were obliged to send a *coolie* to stop the firing until we had passed. The higher we mounted the more eagerly I looked up for some signs of the station, yet it was long before a house was sighted. The first was built on a peak so high above me and so abrupt, that I could not believe it was inhabited. Gradually others appeared, filling me with awe at their position; but as I approached their level they fell into their proper places, and my feelings changed with my own ascent, till I looked down with contempt on the very houses I had looked up to with awe from below. How truly this illustrates the career of many; and probably I might have been inclined to regard my fellow-creatures with the same feelings unless watched and checked, if my ascent in life had been equally rapid.

The bearers toiled up through a thick wood, and suddenly we came on a handsome level road. We had reached the Mall and stood in the centre of the station of Murree.

The sanatorium is elevated more than seven thousand feet above the sea, and is on the high road from Cashmere to the plains of India. It was established on the annexation of the Punjaub, and has since continued to be the convalescent depot for that great province. The Mall passes between and circles round the two peaks bounding the saddle-like ridge where the station stands. The barracks are excellent and picturesquely placed near the centre. Considering the short time, it had been established, the houses were good and the roads excellent.

The bleak winds from the north have left the steep precipices, or *kuds*, as they are called, facing that direction, bare of timber; but on the south side the slopes are densely wooded. The Mall winds through the noble pines of the forest, amid whose branches gambol countless monkeys.

Small paths lead to houses hidden among the tall, straight stems of innumerable pines. Out from the damp and gloomy shade the chief road emerges on the crest, and then the spectator sees the vastness of the Himalayah.

To one thoroughly imbued with the scenery of this region all other mountains sink to insignificancy. The pines struggle up to the crest, and stand erect in defiance of the storm, their branches torn, and here and there their trunks blasted by lightning. The Mall winds round the peak, passing the best houses of the station. The *bazaar* lies below the barracks, and a pretty church stands in a hollow close by, through which the road leads to Cashmere.

The military command is limited to two years, and a subordinate, termed a "Station Staff," is detailed for the same period. The duty officers remain during the season, or hot weather, as well as nearly all the men (selected by the doctors from the European regiments in the province), numbering about four hundred. The command allowance of £20 a month scarcely suffices for the increased expense of every necessary; yet the appointment is eagerly sought, as people pay to go to the hills and consider the permission an indulgence.

The house we were fortunate to secure was rented, unfurnished, at from £100 to £120 *per annum*. In England it would be considered a very small, very badly-built and very inconvenient cottage. As food is dear, and more clothing necessary, higher wages are demanded by the servants; and those who do not bring their own, find it difficult to get any, and impossible to procure good ones. Everything, even water, is carried up the mountain on the backs of men, mules, or camels.

Such transport is always costly, no matter what may be the price of labour, and wine, beer, and all English stores are therefore extravagantly high. Some cases of wine sent up to us from Calcutta cost little short of two shillings for the carriage of each bottle alone; though, I must add, the greater part of this enormous sum was charged by the Ganges Steam Navigation Company for that portion of the transport that ought to have been the cheapest.

We had purchased some furniture and were beginning to feel settled, when a dark cloud gathered over the station. Cholera had been raging in Cashmere, and the doctor reported some cases of a suspicious nature that appeared at the depot.

The dark cloud was a literal fact, as well as a figurative expression, for a column of mist fell over the hill like a pall, penetrating into every house. There it hung like death, stealing around all the contents and spreading over them a green and unhealthy mould. Shoes left for a night looked in the morning as if taken from a vault with the rot of a year on them. Scarcely a breath stirred the leaves—nothing moved except the rain that at intervals fell in torrents. The air was without electricity, without wind and loaded with moisture—we were living in a stagnant cloud.

One day, on my husband's return from the orderly room, I heard that the dire disease had grasped the depot. I was amazed as well as horrified to learn that five men out of the small force were lying in the dead-house; many more were dying, and cases were rapidly filling the hospital. Was it possible? Could this really be the work of a few hours?

Then commenced one of those trying periods well known in India, which we may be thankful Providence has made so short. So malignant was the epidemic at this stage that men attacked could scarcely hope to see the sun go down. Many who rose in what they considered health slept in their graves before night, and it was shocking to learn that the orderly who had carried a message to the house was buried when next inquired for.

Still the pall hung over us—still the rain came. It seemed as if a net had been thrown over the station, and that noxious and deadly gases had been let loose in the atmosphere. On one of the worst days Colonel Muter remained so late at the hospital that I became uneasy and called the *ayah* to help me to prepare for his return. I heaped logs on the fire, rolled the sofa before it, heated blankets, pillows and a Jaeger dressing-gown, ordered plenty of boiling water in which to bathe his feet, and with a bottle of champagne ready and a good-sized goblet, awaited my husband's return. When he appeared I saw how exhausted he was. He said he was not well, but had been obliged to stay as it was necessary at once to disperse the men. I made him lie down in the hot blanketing and pillows before the blazing fire, and after a good draught of the champagne he felt considerably restored, and presently fell into a peaceful, restorative sleep.

Every measure holding out a chance to stay the pestilence was adopted, and fortunately for the poor soldiers, Sir John Lawrence was at the station. This distinguished civilian, who took the liveliest interest in the sufferings of the men, was a constant visitor at the hospital, and cheered, by his presence as well as kind words and acts, the stricken and the dying soldiers.

My husband had the satisfaction of knowing that every means the government could command, every luxury the station could supply, was lavishly bestowed. The first step was to break up the depot, and for this purpose a very large house was given over by order of Sir John Lawrence.

The epidemic was singularly partial in its choice of locality. As usual, it commenced in the hospital, and there was a detached barrack standing near it, in which it proved almost certain death to sleep. The men, being invalids, fell an easier prey, but I doubt whether the epidemic ever showed itself on the plains in a more virulent form than here in a region hitherto considered exempt from such visitations.

Though more than one-sixth of the men were buried before the pestilence left, yet only two of the European residents at the station died. This is often the case on the plains, where it is no uncommon thing to see a number of the soldiers fall victims to cholera, while no other English inhabitant of the cantonment is attacked.

This was the first appearance of cholera at any of the sanitary stations, but these depots had not as yet proved their salubrity. Statistics are liable to error in the results they convey; still there is much point in the fact that not one of these establishments on the peaks of the Himalayah stood at the head of the list of comparative healthiness of Indian stations.

Rawul-Pindee had recorded fewer deaths and a smaller sick-list from an equal number of soldiers than any of these. It may be said that invalids are quartered at the sanatoria, yet there are hill stations with entire regiments, as at Kussowlie and Dugshai, which are not found to be as healthy as Umballa or Rawul-Pindee.

After the Punjaub war my husband's battalion was quartered at Subathoo and Kussowhe, close to Simla, where the men suffered much from sickness. It may be that the seeds of disease were sown in the campaign during which they marched nearly all the way from Kurachee to Peshawur, starting at the end of one hot season and not arriving till the next was well advanced. The soldiers were pleased to find themselves again on the plains; and from what I could gather I conclude they like these hill stations as a change, but not as a quarter for a long period.

The value of these sanatoria is not to be estimated by their comparative salubrity. To the heat-exhausted resident of the cantonment below, the cool and invigorating air must be beneficial; nor is the change confined to the atmosphere. After the monotonous wards of a hospital with its walled enclosure, without a flower—after the interminable flat, with its endless crops and villages—the eye rests with an indescribable relief on the vast mountains and their wild and tangled vegetation.

Though it was the poor soldiers and the natives in the *bazaar* who died, yet few of the people in Murree escaped without an attack of illness. The atmosphere had during this time a power of seizing on any weakness or aggravating any complaint to which a person was liable. I was pained to see how much Colonel Muter's constitution had been affected by exposure in two consecutive hot weather campaigns, and it was with considerable dread I observed his constant attendance in a spot where the plague seemed to have developed all its venom. I could not utter a word of objection to visits to the hospital and barrack-rooms, for no duty could be more clear. Still his health had been so undermined that the risk he ran was much increased, and so was my anxiety.

I had lost faith, after this sad introduction to the command, in the restorative power of the climate of Murree, and I felt a total change of scene was required as well as of climate. I strongly urged, therefore, a return to Europe. My husband was loth to leave the benefits of the appointment it had cost him so much to take up, and the doctors recommended him to wait and try the effects of the cold season. My husband had now attained the brevet rank of Lieutenant-Colonel, awarded for his services in Rohilcund.

The weather that followed in the autumn was charming in the extreme, and the atmosphere assumed the purity and brilliancy of an Italian sky. Then the station became the gayest, the days were enlivened by picnics and many evenings with pleasant little dances. One of these picnics was planned on a large scale for the soldiers, who were to compete for prizes in athletic exercises. The only level ground, about two miles distant, called *Topah*, or the "Flat," was chosen. When on my way there, I inquired why a number of men I passed were returning; I was informed that the camel on whose back the delicacies had been packed had fallen down the *kud*. This was a disastrous end for the plum-puddings and pies I had been manufacturing for days; and

SIR JOHN LAWRENCE

not even the young soldiers for whom they were intended could have grieved more than myself over the loss.

Notwithstanding these little efforts at amusement, the station could not easily shake off the effects of the recent fatal visitation, and soon the people began to hurry back to their work on the plains. One by one, and family by family, they disappeared, and we were left by degrees almost alone on the desolate mountain, amid the forsaken houses.

Before leaving, Sir John Lawrence wrote to Colonel Muter to express the admiration with which he had observed his unwearying efforts to help those under his command during the trying ordeal of malignant cholera; his constant presence in the hospital and cheery manner having done much to comfort the dying, and to sustain and promote the recovery of those not hopelessly smitten.

As the season progressed the air became extremely rare and even difficult to breathe; icicles formed and snow fell. We watched the "Black Forest" mountain that faced us and gave the first indication of the approaching winter. A grey sprinkling first appeared, streaked more boldly in white lines on the dark colouring of the tree tops. Perceptibly it spread, until a great field of snow coldly glittered on this high elevation, ten thousand feet above the sea. Then it stole down the sides; lower peaks showed similar signs; we were scarcely conscious that our own summit was streaked in like manner with white. The vales below put on the spotless mantle, and the whole country around was clad by degrees in an icy covering. The snow thickened on the roads, the forest bent under its weight, individual trees sparkled as if encrusted with diamonds, and festoons of icicles hung from the roofs.

Now I saw hoary winter for the first time. In England we see boisterous winter—gloomy, sullen, and wet—but never this. The sun shone as brightly as before, the whole landscape glittered in a manner not to be described, and all the gems in the world, grouped into one mass, could not equal the effulgence of a single tree, when its icy coat was lighted into dazzling brightness by the rays of the sun. Could anyone believe this to be India? Was it not rather Siberia or Spitzbergen?

The houses, built for summer, not for winter, were scarcely habitable, and whole trunks of trees were insufficient to give heat to a room beyond a few feet from the fire. Here was a Christmas region for Anglo-Indians to revel in! and on Christmas Day all who remained at Murree dined together.

That night when we regained our home, a work of no small difficulty in such weather, a bugle rang out the alarm. My heart sank at the sound, and the horrors that had followed it on May 10th passed like phantoms before my mind. As I looked in the direction of the barracks, whither my husband had hurried, a bright glare told that a portion of the building was on fire. The relief was inexpressible when I learnt it arose from a simple cause. The men had been heaping up a Christmas fire till the beams in the roof which projected into the flue caught the flame, and the shingles were soon in a blaze. The Seikhs who were quartered in an adjoining building, were alarmed at the thought of being suspected, and none were more active than they in extinguishing the flames.

I wonder if there is any station in India on which a shade from the great nightmare that passed over the land—the Mutiny—has not fallen. Even Murree, secluded in the hills, has its own tale. The Paharrees (hill men) had assembled in the thick forest below to attack the station, and they advanced through this cover against some houses lying on the outskirts. They were met and defeated by a few armed residents and invalid soldiers, and in this affair some men were killed and others taken and hanged.

The doctor, who had waited to see the effects of this period, now strongly recommended my husband to proceed to England, and this was confirmed by a board, and sanctioned by the commander-in-chief.

I was sorry to leave without visiting Cashmere, as I had heard much of the beauty of that romantic valley. An interdict had been placed on the district, arising from the universal cause of agitation and strife. It is within nine days' journey by narrow, precipitous paths in a dandy, a conveyance consisting of a blanket slung on a pole.

A depot had been established at Murree for the sale of its shawls, but the prices were high, and the shop was only open during the summer.

Snakes and scorpions are numerous at Murree, and in the winter bears and hyaenas often enter the station. There are pheasants and junglefowl in the wood, and at the foot of the hills, black partridge, hares, and pea-fowl. Tigers have been fatal, and a predecessor in the command had been killed by one. There are some good *parseer* in the streams, a fish that attains a large size, and readily takes a fly.

America has extended her mission to this region, and a few of its members were studying the dialects before penetrating into Central Asia. The *dak* bungalows throughout India afford proof of the usefulness of this Moravian Mission, for the traveller will find in each, a neat case of well-assorted religious works. We obtained from this source, to

168

which I had subscribed a small sum, many excellent books of travels and history at a low price, published in Philadelphia.

Perhaps my last act at Murree was to write a letter of apology under circumstances that illustrate the difficulty of comprehending the working of the native mind. All the water for the house had to be carried by a *bheestie* (a water carrier) up a steep path from a well far down the hillside. To save him this toil we bought a bullock with the necessary skins. No sooner did the *bheestie* see it than with tears in his eyes he begged to be left to his work and not compelled to adopt a new way, adding that he would double the quantity if required. I explained it was solely for his benefit the purchase had been made, but he was not happy till the animal had been expelled.

Part 5: Return to England—Wreck by Fire in the "Eastern Monarch"

CHAPTER 11

I left Murree on December 31st, 1858, a few days before my husband was ready, as it was feared a fall of snow might shut up the road, and I remained at the house of a friend at Rawul-Pindee till he had finished his business with the depot. Our baggage had been forwarded to Jhelum, whither we followed almost immediately after.

The cantonment of Jhelum escaped ruin, as the mutineers had not held it while in open rebellion, yet it was the scene of one of the fiercest struggles of the Mutiny. A portion of the 24th, under Colonel Ellis, with some guns, were sent to disarm the native troops. The *sepoys* took to their huts, and from this cover opened a heavy fire upon the British soldiers. When driven from their shelter, they fell back on another line and the fighting continued among the houses all day with heavy loss of life. Before the natives were expelled, the colonel with scores of his men had fallen.

Not far from this spot, so near, indeed, as to be within sound of the cannon, is situated another field on the banks of the Jhelum. Only a few years had elapsed since the soldiers of this regiment lay there dead in hundreds. Seldom, indeed, even in British fights, had a battalion of our army suffered to a like extent, for half the officers engaged were killed, and nearly all the other half were wounded; while more than five hundred wearing the uniform of the 24th lay strewn on the ground of Chillianwallah. It will be long ere this field is forgotten in the annals of that regiment.

We found the deputy-commissioner had prepared two boats for our passage down the stream. These large flat-bottomed craft are engaged by measurement and then fitted with a mat-house, according to the purse and fancy of the traveller. The mat-house erected on that for us had a sitting-room, a bedroom and a bath-room; the other, a kitchen and a servants' room. Stock is laid in as for a voyage, and the boats float down the broad stream day after day, mooring, or *lagowing*, as it is termed, during the night. Heavy clouds hung over the hills, and it was raining fast when we started. At night the river rose, and before daylight the bank where we moored was inundated, and we were swept down like chips in a current. As we dashed along in the grey light of early dawn, we saw the people of a village working hard to remove their property. Masses of the bank were tumbling down and the interior of some of the houses was exposed to view. How unpleasant must be a residence in a situation so precarious!

The salt ranges to the right, though a mine of wealth to the government, looked barren and desolate. From these mines—of course, a government monopoly, as is all salt in the country—the supply is extracted for the inhabitants of this portion of India; and it can be traced a vast distance over the provinces, till it reaches a boundary line where that from the sea comes into competition. A few miles to the left lay the celebrated battleground of Chillianwallah, with the heights Shere Singh had held, rising abruptly, and showing signs that the river had once flowed at their feet, though now some two or three miles from its bed. The Seikhs fought with these precipices and this river in their rear, and had Lord Gough succeeded in his plan, which was only frustrated by a wise movement on the part of his adversary, nothing more would have been heard of the Khalsa Army.

Beyond the height, near a village which has given its name to the field, a tall column rises from the spot where a legion of England's finest soldiers lie buried—the fatal and almost the only result of that disastrous action.

When darkness settled on the river, we *lagowed* and walked on shore, then retired to rest, and started again at daylight. The boatmen do not trouble themselves much by rowing, the water rolling on between three and four miles an hour, and often rushing down a rapid at far greater speed. Thus, we generally accomplished some fifty miles in the day. It occasionally blew fresh across the stream, and then we were driven against the bank, our boat being as unmanageable as that of a schoolboy. The crews, quite satisfied, would go on shore and gather sticks to prepare their dinners, when no goading on our part had any effect. We proceeded in this manner for days, with little to interest us save the flights of birds and the drowsy crocodiles basking in the sun.

We passed into the Chenab, and as the stream from the junction continues to be called by that name the greater river is lost in the lesser. Then we received the waters of the Ravee, and next day reached Moultan, the highest spot then connected with the sea by steam.

The arrival and departure of vessels is uncertain, and we were compelled to take our chance, though we had tried to obtain information to guide our departure from Murree. Our disappointment was great to learn that a steamer had just left, and that it would be many days before another arrived.

The cantonment, like every place of importance on the river, is several miles from its banks. The Indus has no regularly-cut channel. It courses over a wide expanse to the sea, and all Scinde may be said to be its bed. The heavy splash of its falling banks never ceases, as the winding river, deserting its channel, seeks a new one in the cultivated country. Then the capricious water meets with an impediment, after destroying the villages and fields for scores of square miles, and turns back over the course it had vacated when green with grain and covered with villages, and goes *splash—splash—splash*—till it sweeps them all from the face of creation. Nowhere in the neighbourhood will this tyrant allow a town to arise whose foundation is not guaranteed by a rocky charter, against which the river frets and fumes in vain.

Sometimes its waters take a savage revenge, as at Tatta, by leaving the city, whose prosperity had been connected with its proximity, isolated in the desert. Such a river in England would require a code of laws, and furnish work for a second Lincoln's Inn, for I believe it to be beyond the power of engineering.

We had no alternative but to remain, and we tried to obtain shelter nearer than the cantonment. My husband, who had landed with this object, returned to show me a house he thought might answer. When I saw the ruin, I concluded he must be joking, as it was simply a shell without roof or doors. Our boathouses were made to supply these deficiencies, and the place assumed something of a habitable form. At night, when the lights were extinguished, the wild animals, to whom the place really belonged, came in wonder to ascertain the cause of the strange change. Wolves scratched at the doors, jackals howled outside, and an unknown creature, supposed to be a wild-cat, bounded across the room. I rose and dressed to prepare for the arrival of visitors of greater pretensions. As we decided this place would not do, we made a move to secure a more substantial shelter in the cantonment, the more so as our gipsy home would have been a still poorer defence against the storm that threatened than against the original inhabitants.

We met with a kind reception from a stranger, who placed a vacant bungalow at our disposal; and it was well we did not delay, for a cloud of dust swept over the station, followed by rain that inundated the country.

I took much interest in a visit to the fort, as Colonel Muter had been present at the siege and capture in 1848-49. The carnage during the siege had been frightful, heaps of mangled bodies about the town bore witness to the effects of British ordnance; yet more stood to be shot down or bayoneted in the streets. Moolraj was still in the citadel with some thousands of his best fighting men, and the fort guns were used as vigorously as ever. Kaye writes:—

The strength of this terrible fortress seemed to laugh our breaching batteries to scorn. Mining operations were therefore commenced, but carried on, as they were, beneath a constant discharge from our mortars, it seemed little likely that the enemy would wait to test the skill of the Engineers. The terrible shelling to which the fortress was exposed dismayed the pent-up garrison. By January 21st, 1849, they were reduced to the last extremity. Moolraj vainly endeavoured to rally his followers. Their spirit was broken. There was nothing left for them but to make a desperate sally and cut their way through the besiegers, or to surrender at once.

The noble alternative was rejected. Asking only for his own life, and the honour of his women, Moolraj tendered on that day his submission to the British general. Whish refused to guarantee the first, but promised to protect the women, and on the following morning the garrison marched out of Moultan, and Dewan Moolraj threw himself on the mercy of the British Government. The surrender set free some 62,000 men, and Whish marched to the banks of the Jhelum to swell the ranks of the grand army.

The road is pretty, but the site of the fort was a huge mound with a mosque standing on the crest and some of the bomb-proofs that furnished so poor a defence from our shells, to the followers of Moolraj. Every trace had disappeared of those towering walls, whose triple row had rendered this citadel famous as a place of strength. Runjeet Singh had lost an army before his flag floated from the spot where I stood, and for months the ground around was occupied by the formidable force brought against it by the British before they became masters of the place.

My husband could scarcely fix the direction of the approaches—although he had seen many a gallant soldier fall in carrying up the sap, and the circumstances of a first campaign remain strongly fixed in the memory, so completely had the fort of Moultan disappeared.

At Goojerat, where a battle followed, after our victory at the siege of Moultan, for the first time Seikh and Afghan were banded together against the British power; and, in the words of Lord Dalhousie, the action was memorable alike from the greatness of the issues involved as from the brilliant and decisive result:—

> It was an occasion which demanded the putting forth of all the means at our disposal, and so conspicuous a manifestation of the superiority of our arms as should appal each enemy, and dissolve at once their compact by fatal proofs of its futility. The completeness of the victory won equalled the highest hopes entertained.

Kaye continues:

> At Goojerat, Lord Gough fought a great battle as a great battle ought to be fought. Every arm of the fine force was brought into play. From early dawn on that bright morning the cannonade commenced. The Bengal Artillery made a noble display. Resolute and well handled, the Seikh Army could not stand up against the steady fire. By noon the enemy were retreating in disorder; their positions carried, their guns, ammunition, camp equipage, and baggage captured, their flying masses driven before their victorious pursuers, from midday receiving severe punishment in their flight. And all this was accomplished with little loss of life on the side of the victors.

A division under Sir Walter Gilbert, in which was the 60th Royal Rifles, was ordered to follow up the success of Goojerat and to drive the Afghans from the Punjaub:—

> By a series of rapid marches, scarcely excelled by any recorded in history, the enemy were convinced of the hopelessness of further resistance. The Barnszye force fled before our advancing columns, and secured the passage of the Khybur before British influence could close it against the fugitives. By the Seikhs themselves the game had been clearly played out. The Khalsa

was now quite broken; Shere Singh had nothing to do but to trust the British Government.

On March 5th, 1849, the British prisoners were sent safely into Sir Walter Gilbert's camp. On the 8th he appeared in person to make arrangements for surrender, and on the 14th the remnant of the Seikh Army, some 16,000 men, including thirteen Sirdars of note, laid down their arms at the feet of the British general.

A Proclamation was issued announcing that the kingdom founded by Runjeet Singh had now come under British rule.

The country that had passed by right of conquest into our hands comprised fifty thousand square miles, and contained a population of about four millions, composed of Hindoos, Mahomedans, and Seikhs. It was a Seikh Government we had supplanted, and mainly a Seikh army we had conquered. But the cities of the Punjaub, as this territory is called, after its Five Rivers— were Mahomedan cities, and even before Delhi had become the Imperial City of the Moguls, Lahore had been the home of the Indian kings. The fertile province of the Punjaub has proved of the greatest value to the British Government, and hence, too, we drew our Seikh reinforcements, who aided us so materially in our operations before Delhi.

Moultan was the scene of one of those singular outbreaks during the Sepoy Revolt that, for their folly, could only have excited the derision of the world, had they not been attended with such fearful tragedies. Two disarmed native regiments had remained there quietly until scarcely a vestige was left of the revolution except the vast political ruin it had wrought. The soldier had accomplished his work, all but the final chase, leaving to the monster the life of a hunted hare, and every double seemed to be his last.

At this stage, late in 1858, these regiments conceived the project of raising anew the monster's head. Had they seen something of the appalling nature of the work they proposed, in the fields of bones whitening in the North-West Provinces, the desolation that had fallen on their fair cities, even they might have shrunk from the task. Had they known the hecatombs of their kind that had perished in the vain attempt—the number of princes and peasants that had died on the gallows, victims to their ignorance of England and the English—they must have drawn back, if rational men or beings capable of learning from experience. Failing this knowledge, it is strange that instinct should not have told them the attempt was certain to be at once fatal

SIR HENRY LAWRENCE

to themselves.

A battery of the Royal Artillery, the 1st Bombay Fusiliers, and an Irregular Cavalry regiment were quartered in the barracks. The plan was to rush into the rooms of the infantry soldiers while the men lay drowsily on their beds during the heat, to seize on their arms, and to possess themselves of the guns. They were persuaded that the cavalry were more likely to act with than against them, and they hoped, after cutting to pieces the Europeans in the station, to form a complete and powerful brigade, with which to march straight against Lahore.

An eye-witness informed us that just before the midday gun—the appointed signal—he heard some sinister rumours in the *bazaar* that induced him to proceed towards the European lines. When it was fired, he saw the *sepoys*, armed with every weapon they could appropriate—and the number, in spite of precautions, was considerable—rush with loud cries on the barracks of the Fusiliers.

A moment like this comprises years of life. When fortune or ruin rests on one of the horses speeding together to the winning-post, the person whose interest is involved may experience a painful excitement, but what can that be compared to this?—life and all being the stake at issue. The head of the column was entering the verandah; already the sticks and swords were raised to strike, when it was thrown back like a surging wave on a rockbound coast, and from every window streamed a fire that scattered to all points the native host.

That the soldiers alone should have been prepared is another instance that England owes much to their vigilance. So completely was the Punjaub taken by surprise, that it is asserted the order from the chief commissioner to re-arm these regiments was actually at the time in the station.

The adjutant of the fusiliers was met and murdered, and the bands of the *sepoys* carried terror and consternation wherever they spread. People living a short way off had to fly for their lives, and all hung in suspense till the conduct of the cavalry was decided. This regiment was quickly mounted and drawn up under its officers, who decided for them if they ever did waver. Many *sepoys* died under the sabres of the *sowars*, perhaps before they recovered from their astonishment at the hand that struck the blow. The two regiments perished to a man! The country became a large grave, and the world would have looked on aghast at the spectacle had not the enormous crimes, sufferings and death involved in the revolt accustomed it to such scenes.

A few telegrams and letters copied from the Indian into the English newspapers was all the notice accorded to a Mutiny more sanguinary than that of Barrackpore, more fatal than that of Vellore, which have furnished pages for history and matter for generations to discuss.

The magnitude of events may fairly be judged by the notice accorded to each act. A battle in the later wars of Napoleon, where ten thousand soldiers fell, is treated as an affair of advance guards, and the extent of the great uprising in India may be estimated by the manner in which the inundation dwarfed heights Nature intended for mountains. So, this business, in which, a few weeks before, hundreds upon hundreds of men had perished, was almost lost in the tragic acts that so thickly preceded it.

Chapter 12.

We embarked on the steamer *Havelock*, one of the East India Company's boats, where the cabins are few and small, the ladies only sleeping in them, the gentlemen always, when afloat on the coast or on the rivers of India, making a bed for themselves under the awning on deck. The run is made in daylight, and with great care, for, in a river such as I have described, a vessel may be unable to get down a channel she had a few hours before come up. Miles of sandbanks, rising just above the water, occupy the centre of its bed, and it is most difficult to tell through which channel the main body flows. When the snows of the Himalayah in the hottest months melt, the tide of the Indus sweeps over these sandbanks, and occupies the whole channel till the water is almost on a level with the bank, and the traveller in midchannel sees nothing but a boundless sea in swift motion around him.

With all their care, the steamers often ground, and one morning when at breakfast—hot tea, poached eggs and savoury stews distributed—the steamer struck with such violence that we were thrown down in a row on each side of the table and the tea, crockery, and eggs fell in showers over us, one gentleman only, whose chair was supported by an iron stanchion, remaining a spectator of our fall.

The Indian Navy, with a noble confidence in human nature, makes it the interest of the captains of these boats to be as long as possible on the passage, a principal portion of the pay of these gentlemen being derived from a contract for the supply of the passengers with food *per diem* instead of by the passage.

The day after our departure we reached the Punjaub, as the Five Streams are termed, from where the Sutlej joins, to their junction with the Indus at Mittancote. There is no stream of any importance that flows into the Indus from Mittancote to the sea. In fact, the country below that town is a thirsty desert, except along the banks of the river, which supplies the arid soil with water. The river therefore loses greatly in its course to the sea, the body of water at Mittancote being much larger than at Tatta. To me the country wore a wretched aspect. The distant hills were low, tame, and barren, the banks level and monotonous, the mud-houses mere hovels, the stretches of the bare sand interminable, or covered with a low green shrub. Sukkur, with its island fort of Bukkur, and the singular town of Rooree, with its strange rocks, forms the only spot of beauty.

The river has here burst through a range of hills, and these buildings are perhaps the most secure from attack on the side towards the sea. After taking in cargo we started again. Among the passengers was a Scindian convict, who had murdered his wife, a crime prevalent in the country, and one with which the magistrates have found difficulty; as the husband, regarding the English law an unjustifiable interference with his rights, compelled the wife to hang herself.

We found a "flat" full of passengers waiting at Kotree to be towed to Kurrachee. Kotree is the terminus of the Scinde Railway, which connects the port at Kurrachee with the Indus at Kotree, but at that time unfinished.

I regretted to leave the river without tasting *pulla*, a fish said to be most delicate, captured in great numbers during the season by men, who float down the stream on red earthen jars called *chatties*, with a triangular net at the end of a pole. The fish heading upstream strike against the net, are caught and deposited in the chatty. The expertness of these fishers on their *chatties*, borne on the rapid and most dangerous stream, surprises the lookers-on.

When we got out to sea the salt water mixing with the fresh in the boilers checked the power of generating steam to a degree I had no idea of, and it was not till the fresh water had been expended that the vessel resumed her due speed.

I was charmed once more to see the blue ocean; those only can tell how much, who have been encompassed with the dangers that surrounded me hundreds of miles from its shore, and it was with the sea I had always associated safety and the power of my country.

A few hours' steaming brought us from the mouth of the river to the harbour of Kurrachee.

Kurrachee lies to the left of a low line of barren and arid hills, offshoots of the great chains of Central Asia, which attain their highest grandeur in the vast Himalayah. The country around is a dreary plain of sand, broken by white hillocks drifted in long ridges. The harbour is formed by a headland, the last promontory of the mountains, called Minora Point. The elevation is a few hundred feet, falling precipitously into the sea, where the water reaches its greatest depth. From Minora a dreary waste of mud and sand is seen, with a few rocks near the entrance of the harbour, standing up like ships at sea.

At the full the tide invades the desert, and the white sand sparkles in bright contrast with the blue water, but at the ebb, the reaches of mud seem endless. The harbour is safe, but there is a bar at the entrance, which excludes vessels of large size. Its left side is formed by a *bundur*, built by Sir Charles Napier, which runs from the town for a considerable distance, connecting it with an island nearly opposite Minora, and on the right side looking seaward is Minora and its spit. The town, whose wretched hovels are in keeping with the miserable country, stands at the head of the harbour on debris rising out of the mud, a mere fishing village, for fish abound in the waters.

The cantonment is three miles inland, and is rapidly assuming the dimensions of a city. The clear judgment of Sir Charles Napier foresaw the destiny of the place, and perhaps never before had the eye of a founder of a commercial emporium looked on a more uninviting site. Yet Kurrachee is destined to a great future; indeed, to a rivalry with the chief ports of trade; and if the harbour does not fill up, it requires little spirit of prophecy to foretell that a second Bombay will arise at this outlet of the Indus. (I am told this forecast has been realised since the above was first written in my journal early in 1859.)

Colonel Muter had some years before been quartered in the cantonment, and had many times passed up and down the Indus. Then no ship was seen in the port except war steamers with regiments or with the mails. Now the harbour was crowded with vessels; but all the way down the banks that appeared to me so dreary showed signs to him of a rapid advance. The mountain tribes begin to learn there is more to be obtained by commerce than by war. They had already been taught that little is gained and often much is lost by their inroads into our territory, while by entering into commercial relations with us they find a ready market for articles they had before looked upon as valueless.

Nowhere in the world (1911) are the exports increasing with greater speed. The linseed, grain, and flax of the Punjaub are only a portion of the vast trade destined to float down the Indus. Wool has become a staple, and, no doubt, the pastoral tribes will add to this ex-

180

port, skins, tallow, and all the produce of stock, and of the wealth that has its origin in grass.

CHAPTER 13

The invalids who had left the Punjaub long before us were awaiting the arrival of a ship taken at Bombay for their conveyance home. This vessel, called the *Eastern Monarch*, was said to be the finest merchant-ship afloat, and we hoped to obtain a passage in her, there being little chance of securing one for a lady by the Overland route, as the cabins in those steamers had been engaged for several mails.

When the *Eastern Monarch* was signalled, my husband proceeded to her anchorage outside the harbour, as she drew too much water for the bar. He had a race out to secure a cabin, and the following day we embarked with the troops in a small steamer. The great teak East Indiaman lay at anchor without a motion, while the steamer was pitching and rolling in the swell, and she dare not go alongside; we were, therefore, transferred by boats, a most unpleasant operation, and not without danger, as one of the boats was sunk, and the occupants nearly drowned.

I was delighted when I stood on the poop of the noble *Eastern Monarch* calmly riding to her anchor, while the little steamer rolled heavily and the *pattama* she had towed out full of soldiers was pitching frightfully and grinding itself to pieces against the ship's side.

On the evening of February 22nd, 1859, the vessel dropped her topsails and stood out to sea, and I well remember the chorus that rose from many happy hearts as the dreary shores of Beloochistan faded away:—

Oh! stay, stay, stay"—"No, no—no; no,
For the sails are spread, and away we go,
And now we're bound for England, ho!

Light winds baffled us during the first part of the voyage, and while we lay on the water like a log, we saw the steamer as she crossed swiftly to Aden with some of our fellow-passengers of the *Havelock* onboard. The wind freshened after crossing the Line, and we doubled the Cape in beautiful weather on April 8th. Ten days more brought us to St. Helena, a few hours after a passenger ship from Calcutta had secured every means of conveyance to Long wood and Napoleon's Tomb. I had then either to walk or give up the idea of visiting these celebrated spots. The road leads along the barren hillside from the deep gully where Jamestown nestles, but as it approaches the top it becomes wooded, and opens a vast prospect of the sea. Before I gained the summit, I found the difficulty of the task I had undertaken on a bright day in a tropical climate, but the glorious trade-wind came blowing freshly over the hill when I arrived at the top.

The house once occupied by Napoleon stands on a grassy plateau ventilated by the perpetual breezes of the South-east Trade, and looks down on the stream of ships that flow by on their passage to Europe and North America.

The French had charge and were collecting materials for the repair of the house, then in a most dilapidated state. The situation is healthy and not wanting in beauty.

At the foot of one of the abrupt hollows of this lonely and pre-cipitous island we entered the tomb which once contained all that remained of the great emperor. The vegetation at this spot—for St. Helena—is considerable, but my husband looked with surprise at the renowned willow, the venerated parent of some slips brought by French emigrants to New Zealand, where they had grown into great trees, under whose luxuriant shade he had often bathed in a mountain stream running into the lovely harbour of Akaroa.

Since this visit a change has been effected at Longwood, which has resumed the same habitable condition as when occupied by the mighty genius who there fretted out his life. No more the profane foot of the English traveller may desecrate the tomb where the great warrior lay, for the French have erected a solid arch of masonry to cover the sacred soil.

On our return we found the captain at the hotel, anxious to get to sea, as the arrival of two such fine ships had roused the innate love of the English for a fair bet, and the people of St. Helena were laying large sums on the arrival in England first of the *Agamemnon* or the *Eastern Monarch*. We had seen the *Agamemnon* get under way, and with surprising speed spread a cloud of canvas to the breeze; but though it was late that night when the *Eastern Monarch* started, we passed her about half-way to Ascension.

The only bad weather we experienced was off the Azores, and there would have been little to cloud the monotonous smoothness of the voyage had it not been for the frequent deaths among our poor invalid soldiers.

The Indian Government dealt most liberally with its disabled and worn-out troops, in its last act, before it turned them on the wide world. The finest ships that could be procured—the most ample space, light, and ventilation—the best medical attendance, comforts, and even luxuries, were amply supplied. What a pity the lavish expenditure should stop here, and the man on whom such care had been bestowed should be found shortly afterwards starving in the streets of London! There were many debilitated by the climate whose constitution could not be renewed, and they sank by degrees and died, some victims to their own intemperance, but others, alas! to the year too long in India. Men in the last stages of disease are often put onboard to give the only chance of recovery, though the doctors have hardly a hope; but they humour their patients, who to a certainty when left behind, were left, as they know and feel, to die. Thus, we had at sea men destined to a grave in the Southern Ocean, and seventeen were buried before we reached the Cape.

As we neared the English Channel the *Eastern Monarch*, always clean and beautiful, began to grow bright with French polish and paint. The scraping, holy-stoning and redecorating gave us a pleasant feeling of approaching home. One of the first objects we saw as we drew in to shore was the long hull of the *Agamemnon*, and although in the stretches on opposite tacks—for the wind was easterly—she was often lost sight of, yet a day never passed without our seeing her now ahead, then astern, and it was clear the race would be a close one.

At Torbay a fishing-boat came alongside, and my husband proposed to land and proceed by train to London. This course was referred to the captain, who advised us to remain till the ship reached the Isle of Wight, adding that though easterly winds had set in, he would be able with the tide to work rapidly up the coast when he got the pilot on board.

On June 2nd we were beating off the Isle of Wight and stood in close to the shore. How barren the sea-board of other lands look when compared with that of England! Those who see for the first time such a country from the deck of a ship must be charmed with the surprising cultivation presented by every promontory.

The land was intersected by lines cutting its surface into squares chequered like a chessboard and the colours were the green of grass, the varying hue of growing grain, and the dark brown of well-ploughed soil. The country rose and fell in graceful undulation—with clumps of trees, with white winding roads, with towns peeping from hollows and villas nestling in foliage. After other realms it was a garden, not a storm-racked coast.

The captain, having resolved to anchor at Spithead for fresh meat and vegetables, steered for Portsmouth after clearing the point, the ultimate destination for the invalids being Gravesend—very appropriately.

The last vessel whose signals the *Eastern Monarch* was destined to answer was H.M. Screw Transport *Simoon*, that steamed past us for Gravesend. She had left Bombay with the invalids from that Presidency three weeks before we had left Kurrachee, and the captain was pleased to have outstripped this ship, with the advantage of steam, by so long a period.

Next day we were to land, and our trunks were packed and ready to hand over the side. I retired to rest earlier than usual, anticipating fatigue and excitement. As I left the deck the ship was moving gently through the water on that calm summer's evening with the distant and hazy outline of land around.

About midnight I heard the cables as they ran out with that rumbling sound and tremulous motion by which we know that the heavy anchor of a large ship is "let go," telling us that our voyage was accomplished and we had safely reached England. Few, I imagine, can hear that sound without emotions of thankfulness for escape from perils past, and for blessings received, but ours was not an ordinary return. How many had perished during the dreadful commotion through which we had been preserved? After a few solemn and grateful thoughts, I again fell asleep.

While my thoughts were roving back over dangers past how little I suspected that the greatest peril I ever encountered was then kindled beneath me! My mind turned to battles, massacres and cold-blooded murders. Did no shadow fall across it of explosion and fire and shipwreck?

Never while I live, and my senses remain, can I forget my next awakening. The whole ship seemed shattered to fragments; did I dream, or was it indeed a reality? I was hurled from my bed and I stood in the darkness of death. Is it the sea that bursts in a dense volume into the cabin? The decks seem to reel and quiver, to rise and fall. Stifled, I gasped for breath, the air was charged with sulphur, and the atmosphere such that it was death to remain. My mind became a moving panorama. The pictures are now indistinct, but how vividly my whole life passed on the shifting scenes, with one dread certainty that it was death that was now dropping the curtain on my earthly stage. The most distinct feeling I remember of this moment of painful existence was—that this was death. Still, the whole period of the trance was but a moment; then instinct took the place of shattered reason, and it is astonishing how rightly it guides.

I found my hand on the door; by a great effort I pushed it open, and a rush of fresh air cleared away from my brain much of the shock from which I was suffering. Immediately my husband was standing by my side, and amidst the stillness that followed I heard his voice, as he called loudly to those on deck to raise the skylights. The cuddy was in utter ruin, the tables shattered, the chairs broken, and the place strewn with fragments of glass. At my feet an awful chasm yawned. Far down I could see a bright glare that told the ship was on fire.

The explosion had passed close to where we slept, torn up the decks, both this and that beneath, and blown away the after-companion ladder by which we gained the poop. Fragments of the brass balusters alone hung down, which my husband seizing, by a vigorous effort, he gained the poop; then stooping down he grasped my upraised hands, and in a few minutes, I was lifted to the top. I felt as if the weight of worlds was in my limbs, and that I was powerless to struggle against the mountain crushing me down. My mind was keenly active, though my body was powerless, and I was conscious it required the greatest exertion to raise me to the deck; yet I could do nothing to assist myself, though vividly aware of the awful fiery chasm down which I would be precipitated if my husband failed in his effort.

The change was more than earthly when I stood on the deck, breathing the pure air, and looking on the tranquil shore of England, quietly resting on this balmy morning in the moon's soft light. I was there before the ship recovered from the shock; but then arose the wildest screams, and a tumult burst forth as if Bedlam had broken loose. I heard Colonel Muter give directions to a soldier who had rushed up, and I saw him grasp the arm of a man who staggered as if he would fall, and place him on a seat. This was the pilot, who had left the deck but an hour before for his first sleep for nights, when he was blown from the cuddy-table, where a bed had been made for him through the skylight up to the poop.

My husband then went to the poop-rail and assumed command:—

"Men, fall in at once for parade; get the buckets in order; don't crowd the gangways; cut down the ropes; lower yourselves to the water; you will be picked up by the boats," etc., etc.

Thus, all panic was arrested, and, with the exception of seven, chiefly among the women and children, killed in the first explosion, then close upon a thousand invalid soldiers, many of whom had not left their hammocks during the voyage, got safely to land. Meanwhile my husband had groped back to our cabin, and Captain Stopford of the 52nd, one of our fellow-passengers, came to tell me of his danger, and that if I called to him, I would induce him to return to deck. He came, panting from the smoke, but partially dressed, and asked if he could easily get anything of value.

I said, "Yes." I had seventeen sovereigns at hand, which I had procured in exchange for *rupees* before leaving India. He got them, and, seizing his hand, I asked Captain Stopford to take the other, to prevent his return to the cabin. My husband then got a boat, in which he placed me, with directions to take me and the other two ladies with their children to the *Falcon* man-o'-war. Dr. Kidd, our surgeon, who exerted himself to such good purpose to the rescue of the invalids, threw his military cloak over my shoulders, and Sergeant Mars, who had been under Colonel Muter's command at Murree, said, "I see, ma'am, your feet are bleeding; will you put on a pair of ammunition boots and socks?"

My husband remained on board, and gave valuable assistance in saving life. Being on "sick leave," he was not on any recognised duty, but was ever ready to help to the utmost in his power.

By degrees, the full reality of the perilous position came before me. The ship had in its cargo two hundred tons of saltpetre. What if another explosion should blow the ship into fragments! The dim coast was miles away, the fire rapidly gaining, and several hundred human beings on board. "Can all be saved?" I mentally exclaimed. "How dreadful the scene will be as it draws to its close." To add to the alarm a woman of unsound mind ran up the main gangway uttering fearful cries. I turned towards her, and saw she carried a child charred to a cinder. "It is not yours!" exclaimed a soldier near. She immediately placed the little corpse on the deck and speeded down for her own little boy.

Away, over the surface of the water, I could discern two or three small craft, and about half-a-mile off lay the black hull of a man-o'-war steamer. My eyes were fixed on this vessel. With delight I observed that the men on board were in rapid motion, and that boats were dropping into the water. Suddenly a light flashed over the sea, a flame burst from her port, followed by the loud roar of a heavy gun; then another and another, which rumbled in echoes along the slumbering shore and awoke the inhabitants of Portsmouth. For the first time this sound came with pleasure on my ear, as that of the signal guns of distress, not of the cannon of the enemy, and it spoke in tones of hope, as it broke on that coast always familiar with disaster and quick to rescue.

At first the only boat, except those the sailors had taken, was the cockle-shell of a pilot schooner, which came alongside, and into which the ladies were directed to get. My husband had collected some of my clothes, but I felt unable to put them on, and had no power to carry them.

When I looked back the ship was in a sheet of flame, her ports as large as those of a frigate being lit up with a dazzling glare. The fire had leaped along the rows of hammocks from which the soldiers had sprung on the alarm, and a line of light shot along the water from each port, increasing as it went, till the whole blended into one, leaving all in brightness below and all in darkness above, for a heavy cloud was gathering over the ship. Three thick volumes of smoke rose straight up from her graceful hull, and I could see over the bulwarks the dark forms of men hurrying to and fro in the black shade cast by the gathering cloud. Now and then a flame shot up amid pillars of smoke rising from the hatchways, disappeared as if choked, and then would rise again higher than before.

Gradually, from the after-hatch, the flame became continuous; the glare fell along the upper deck and gave a red, unearthly tinge to the strange shadows retreating before it. Sometimes it leaped aloft to the thick cloud drifting slowly with the wind; then the lurid light was thrown far over sea and land. Dense smoke arose from the hatchway near the forecastle where now were grouped the whole throng of people. The little boats under the bowsprit looked like midges playing about the head of the great Indiaman. I could see figures springing wildly from the ship into the sea, where they were picked up by the boats, which seemed to fear too close a contact.

When I saw how little these boats could accomplish, I watched with an eager anxiety—the anxiety that fixes the eye and clenches the hand—for I knew the time was short. The progress of the fire was appalling. The fitful flames rising from the hatches had become roaring volcanoes, and the water around danced and glowed in a golden light. Higher and higher it sprang—caught the mainmast and ran up aloft, playing gracefully in the rigging of the beautiful ship. The plentiful supply of varnish, French polish and grease on the spars fed the fire, which darted up the mast, ran along the yards, and mingled with the dark cloud above. Then the mizzen caught the flame, the ropes of the ship seemed to bear innumerable little balls of fire, and the rigging was illuminated as if for a holiday.

I turned from this absorbing spectacle and strained my eyes in the direction of Portsmouth. For a moment I could see nothing but countless stars of light, and despair took possession of my mind. Then the light broke gradually on my sight, and I could scarcely control my emotions on beholding a lugger under a press of sail bearing down in the morning breeze. My gaze was fixed on this vessel, and with a beating heart I watched her progress as she came gallantly on. Borne along both by the tide and the breeze, she came swiftly and straight for the *Eastern Monarch*, and turning rapidly under her jib-boom, the order rang out, "Let go the anchor!" which was dropped under the forecastle of the blazing ship.

From every rope, from every projection, and down the sides of the tall Indiaman came tumbling to the deck of the lugger the dense throng of soldiers, and in an incredibly short time the forecastle was deserted and all packed in the barge.

The flame sprang quickly on the foremast and leaped up over the forecastle as if hurrying to seize a prey it feared might escape; but its prey was gone. Already the bleat of the sheep and the scream of the pig were hushed in death; from stem to stern the all-conquering fire had enveloped the ship, and nothing could live on her raging hull.

A beautiful cow and a lovely gazelle were among the animals that perished. When I began to think over the loss of this night, the sad fate of these timid things came distressingly before me, though the noisy pigs might have claimed equal pity. Every effort was made by the lugger to get clear of the furnace alongside which she was anchored, and I held my breath as the ship's mainmast swayed to one side, bowed itself forward, then took a greater bend to the side, and fell with a crash, bringing along with it the mizzen, hissing into the boiling and bubbling water.

For a few minutes the solitary mast stood erect, wrapt in flame, then swayed like its fellows, and like them fell hissing into the water. With the towering spars went the beauty of the scene—the noble vessel was a dismal wreck! But the fire that had consumed the deck, now sprang up from the cargo with still greater violence, and the heat was felt hundreds of yards around. Far off, in the Isle of Wight, and in Hampshire, the people were startled at the illumination over the great arsenal of the British Navy, and many rose to see if it was the light of the morning that burst with so strong a glare into their rooms.

I could scarcely credit the fact that all this was the work of one short hour. These few minutes only were required for the destruction of the finest and strongest of England's merchant ships, and the disembarkation of the seven hundred souls who but an hour before had been quietly sleeping in what now seemed a volcano raging on the sea.

The ladies removed to the *Falcon*, and I had there the joy of meeting my husband, and of hearing that all had been saved except the seven killed by the explosion, and many hurt by the unavoidable accidents inevitable on such occasions.

An officer of rank arrived in a small steamer with orders for the *Falcon* to sink the *Eastern Monarch*. The man-o'-war, whose steam was up, ranging alongside, drove her shot between the wind and water, but the blazing ship lightened as she burnt, and the shot holes in the water-line gradually rose. They were afraid the fiery furnace they failed to sink might break from her cables and drift among the shipping.

Those who ally themselves to the career of a soldier must be prepared for quick and startling changes. After such an unexpected calamity I felt truly thankful for my happy and safe arrival. What a contrast had been effected in a few short hours! Another great peril had been added to those which had so lately encompassed us—another peril encountered and passed—another mercy vouchsafed, and one that deepened my gratitude to the Protecting Hand that had been stretched out in my defence and in that of another life I held so dear.

As I looked out to sea a huge tower of vapour shot into the heavens from the burning ship. The long-dreaded explosion had come at last; the dangerous cargo had ignited, and burst with a force that would have blown the decks into fragments had decks still been there. For two days the ship remained on fire; then it gradually died out, leaving nothing of the noble vessel which had been towed to the shore save a blackened shell stranded on the beach. The last I saw of the ship so long my home was in that tall, sulphurous column which had risen from the mine over which I had calmly slept for many months.

But though in reality I never again saw the ill-fated *Eastern Monarch*, this scene often came back in my dreams. I again trembled at the awful explosion, again listened to the piercing screams, again beheld the busy throng struggling for life, and again witnessed the stern discipline of the army, the authority of the officers, even in this extremity, prevailing. One frightful nightmare settled on my sleep, though it was weeks before I knew the full extent of the shock I had sustained. The nerves, so long strained, seemed unable to bear this pressure, and were, I feared, injured for ever. In that hour years were added to my life.

The people of Portsmouth, deeply interested in the losses of the returned Indian soldiers, came forward to their relief, and several ladies called to offer us their houses and their clothes.

But I was eager to get home, and we hurried up to London that evening, where we found difficulty in obtaining a bed. It was Epsom Race week; the hotels were full, the metropolis thronged. The waiters looked suspiciously at our attire (though we had each bought a ready-made suit at Portsmouth), and I fear their suspicion was confirmed when they saw there was not an article of baggage on the cab. There was something dreary and disheartening beyond expression in such a return to our country. It seemed as if the misfortune which entitled us to the hand of kindness caused us to be shunned where we had most expected to meet with a hearty reception. After driving to many hotels, where we were assured every room had been secured, we left it to the cabman, who took us to the Queen's Hotel in Cork Street, where we procured the accommodation required.

I retired to rest, but not for one moment could I sleep. Though my frame was sinking with fatigue, my thoughts were working in a way I had not before known, and I could but with difficulty refrain from calling aloud when some dreadful picture of the conflagration passed across my mind.

All that night I heard the ceaseless roll of carriages in the distance as the great stream ebbed and flowed along Piccadilly, broken now and then by a louder rattle when a cab went over the pavement of our own street.

We lost everything but life in the wreck.

I rose early, and when the shops opened bought things most essential, got our letters from the agents, and fast as the Great Western Railway could carry me, hastened to my home.